TOFE EVA

EVERYONE HAS A PLAN UNTIL

SH!T

HITS THE FAN

HOW TO NOT BE THE BITCH OF YOUR OWN BRAIN

ADVANCE PRAISE

Professor Peter Reaburn | Sports Science, Bond University

As a highly committed and award-winning tertiary educator and applied sport scientist, I have been involved in working with young men and women for over 30 years. The three factors I love seeing in young people are passion, commitment to a work ethic, and resilience. Tofe Evans stands out as a young man with not only those qualities but as a person committed to helping others bring their dreams to reality through sharing his personal journey. I like that!

Andy Fell | Founder, GiFT631 & #youth4good

For many years I have been a passionate advocate of what I call the *Rhino Rationale*. Rhinos on the move have pace, momentum, and are a powerful force to be reckoned with. They also have tough, thick skin which is at the core of rhino rationale. People who make a real difference have pace, urgency, direction, and focus. They also have resilience and persistence. The ability to pick themselves up when they get knocked down. Tofe is a brilliant example of someone who demonstrates what rhino rationale is about. He is someone who has achieved incredible things both physically and mentally. Even more admirable is his mental strength, firstly to keep going in these extreme physical challenges and secondly and more importantly to come back from adversity and find a sense of purpose to propel his life forward. I admire him for his openness, honesty, and willingness to learn and develop a winning network. He may have stumbled and even fallen but has now risen to reach new heights on his personal journey. I love and admire his big goals, big courage, and big heart.

Peter Watkins | Director, The Mutual Australian

Tofe is an example of the kind of person the world needs more of. A man who accepts responsibility for his life and then takes action to change the areas that are uncomfortable. To deal with anxiety and depression at the same time could be overwhelming, however as Tofe says, be grateful for the lesson and rediscover the magic in giving. Tofe gives back more than most and therein lies the example of how your world will change when you are not your main focus.

Dr. Nigel Farrow | Medical Research for Cystic Fibrosis

Not only is *Everyone Has a Plan Until Sh!t Hits the Fan* a fascinating read, but it is also a window into a journey through the ups and downs of life and how the overwhelming moments can be overcome. Tofe's approach to overcoming adversity through practical resilience is interesting, practical, and thought provoking; this book takes the reader through a unique journey which changes the way we live, work, and play.

Kirstie Ennis | Marine Corp Veteran, Paralympian, World Climber, Amputee

Tofe and I met at an interesting time in both of our lives. I was recovering from mental, physical, and emotional wounds that I suffered from while serving in the United States Marine Corps as a helicopter door gunner in Afghanistan. I was struggling with repurposing Myself, and at the ripe age of 23 was feeling quite lost. I covered up a lot of my problems with "band-aids" and refused to get help until it was nearly too late. My life turned around after the realization that I controlled my circumstances, they do not control me. It took the six inches between my ears and what's behind my rib cage to truly break the chains that were holding me back from the rest of my life. When your head and your heart are in the right place, anything is possible. I do not mean to sound bleak, as I am now a scholar with three master's degrees, am a

Paralympic hopeful, and am seeking to be the first female above the knee amputee to stand on the highest peaks on each of the seven continents. I have been fortunate to be surrounded by people like Tofe who make me want to do better, be faster, and be stronger. We have been on quite the journey together, even though from afar. While we were once sinking, I am proud of the people Tofe and I are now.

Daniel Flynn & Jarryd Burns | Cofounders, Thankyou

Tofe is the real deal. He's an incredibly inspiring guy, having experienced some of darkest places, suffering from anxiety and depression, and now lives a life helping others mentally, physically, and financially through altruistic charity giving. He has been through the ringer and come out the other side with amazing mental toughness that you rarely encounter. An absolute legend!

Dr. Jodie Bradnam | Clinical Psychologist

Tofe's determination, courage, and energy are woven into the pages of this book. He leads by example, sharing powerful, personal lessons from his journey and offering mind hacks to inspire you to take your own leap of faith.

Meghan Jarvis | Founder and CEO, Buzvil & Australian Ninja Warrior

This is a story that is meant for the reader that is ready to journey deep into their soul purpose and be exposed to some vulnerability and truth bombs from a young gentleman who will expand your belief system and enable you to push forward toward your true purpose. It looks at the depth of defeat and the journey to triumph in a deposition that will heighten your awareness to your true-self and soul's purpose with empathy, understanding, and reflections that are conceptualized into life-long lessons that will enable you to grow to new heights. Tofe's writing is through experience; his life story and his aspirations to assist others on their journey is one that I have reflected time and time again on. He is a gentleman that empowers the youth in Australia and young men like him by providing a new template of deep, inspired action toward one's goals. Anyone who has ever delved into the ebbs and flows of life and searched for the meaning within the lessons and the relation toward their true purpose needs not look any further.

Dr. Steve Maraboli | Behavioral Scientist & Best-Selling Author

Tofe Evans' story is one of triumph, wisdom, and the resiliency of the human spirit. His courage and transparency will surely inspire any reader to reach beyond current circumstances and connect with their greatest life.

EVERYONE HAS A PLAN UNTIL
SH!T HITS THE FAN

EVERYONE HAS A PLAN UNTIL SH!T HITS THE FAN

HOW TO NOT BE THE BITCH OF YOUR OWN BRAIN

TOFE EVANS

LIONCREST
PUBLISHING

EVERYONE HAS A PLAN UNTIL SH!T HITS THE FAN
How to Not Be the Bitch of Your Own Brain

ISBN   978-1-5445-1013-2 *Paperback*
       978-1-5445-1012-5 *Ebook*

For the ones who can rise above the turmoil, no matter how bad the situation is.

CONTENTS

Practical Resilience = Adversity * Mindset * Gratitude

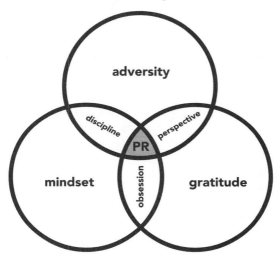

Scan this QR code so we can have you involved in the Facebook Group - Case Studies of Practical Resilience! Believe it or not, your story will experience the Practical Resilience framework and make YOU stronger as a person!

INTRODUCTION

I'VE GOT YOU, GUYS (AND GALS). YOU'RE IN GOOD HANDS!

With almost 130 million books published today, there really isn't a need for another book. Yes, there are selfish reasons to document my legacy, but the core reason I'm writing this is because I genuinely know it could get someone out of a crisis. More importantly, it could save someone from taking their own life.

The journey I've been on these past few years, as well as the achievements I've made in my endurance career, have not only shaped my character, but have saved my life, literally. So, the purpose of this book is to help anyone get out of that deadly, deep, dark rabbit hole called "adversity and suffering." When you think you'll never be able to come out of your situation, I will guide you in the right direction with the lessons I've learned. I've studied, tested, and retested—countless times—those "penny-dropped" philosophical moments of the greats, and I've come out the other side.

Essentially, I'm that war general covered with invisible calluses and scars who will guide you out of the trenches of life and rescue you from the "The Troughs of Sorrow." Honestly, I'm deliberately putting myself into stressful situations every day so that I can really understand the mental game. I'm determined to enter that state of untapped potential, which cultivates the "superhuman" and shows that you can do it too. I truly believe there's a greatness in all of us. We just need to learn how to tap into it.

This book is dedicated to the ones who can rise above the turmoil and any adversity, regardless of your situation; that's the true definition of greatness. What you'll read and endure in the chapters that follow is a culmination of despair, hardships, endurance, and, more importantly, resilience.

It seems we all have a plan when things go right, but how many of us have a plan when things go wrong? Too many people react in such a poor manner, but if they invested in themselves, they'd be proactive with a cool, calm, and collective approach during any turmoil.

It's almost mandatory to have a roadmap to ensure your

vision and purpose transform into reality. However, it's inevitable that you'll come across bumps in the road. As an endurance junkie and limit pusher, this is what I deal with on a day-to-day basis in the field.

I'm not the only one who deals with the struggles of life; you do too. The adversity of breaking up with your partner, a death in the family, or even being stuck in traffic while driving to work are circumstances that are out of your control. Yet, these are the things that make us anxious.

You can be inspired or motivated to a point, but you **MUST** take action **TODAY** to get into the habit of moving forward. Lucky for you, I have included plenty of practical tips throughout this book that will show you what you can do today to begin taking action.

If you are going through a tough time right now, the help I've provided in this book will be your savior. I even show you how to get in touch with me. You can reach out, and I'll be humbled to hear your story. Hopefully, I will meet you one day regardless of where you live.

The world is full of smart people who make the big decisions. Most of the wars (both past and present) happen as a result of calculated planning and execution, which is orchestrated within exceptionally smart minds. These leaders have very strong convictions and they believe their actions are right, even when their intentions are not meant for good. The truth is that it's more about an ego trying to prove who's got the bigger dick. We need smart people because they're finding cures for cancers, solving problems through disruption, and showing what's possible. Though, in this recipe of life, "smart" is severely lacking an ingredient.

So, in saying that, the world needs just as many *kind* people. Wouldn't it be a more pleasant place to live if gratitude was the proponent for kindness (and you'll read more about this throughout the book)? Showing and expressing gratitude over time has a ripple effect that magnifies itself more than most people realize.

If you purchased this book from my site (Tofe-Evans.com/thebook), you'll notice there was no fixed price. It's a "pay-what-you-think-it's-worth" kind of concept. The reasoning for this is it keeps me accountable in releasing a great product and not putting limits on it by having a fixed price. If you pick it up and think it's a useless read, then you'll get a refund. If you think it was decent and worth $50, then pay $50. Or, if you think it's made an incredible impact on how you perceive life, giving you a direction for the greater good, and you feel it's a gift worth $10,000, then that's totally fine too. But, if you're struggling and in dire straits, you can get a copy of the book for free. Yes, I lose money through that purchase, but I'm more focused on transforming those who are feeling weak and worthless into **WARRIORS**—mentally unbreakable, full of purpose, and striving for greatness.

On this project, I have teamed up with LIVIN Org where 10 percent of **ALL** book sales go to a LIVIN program that helps reduce the stigma of mental health, which is becoming very prevalent in the world. The heightened statistics on anxiety, depression, and suicide are insanely scary. As an advocate and spokesperson for mental health, this is something very close to me, and it's an honor to dedicate a portion of the book sales to a cause that'll make this world a better place to live in. I'm a big believer in charity. There's a magic in giving, and I know from my experience that the universe reciprocates in ways you wouldn't imagine. I'm entirely grateful for the journey I've been on, and I want to give back somehow.

To give you some context, I should probably tell you about myself, so you can see if I'm worth a damn. For those of you who give me a chance and take in these lessons with an open mind, I thank you with all my heart. I want you to know that I would love to meet you one day, wherever in the world you are. Otherwise, if you're a black-and-white cynic, close the book up and throw it away, or give it to someone else.

To some, I'm known as that kid who ran a race down the

slopes of Mt. Everest, but most of the time, I get called "crazy" or "fucking nut case" more times than my name. It's all for the right reasons though. As a firm believer of pushing the boundaries of what the human mind and body can handle, I'm constantly reinventing myself to advocate how anyone can get out of any mental rut and be the best version of themselves.

I've designed the material in this book so that each chapter starts with a journal entry from pivotal moments in my life to help you understand and visualize what I was feeling during that time. You'll see that through my dynamic concept of Practical Resilience, each journal entry shifts toward the greater good and will have you wondering whether it can be done for you. **OF COURSE, IT CAN!** But you have to be willing to listen and take in methods that may seem counterintuitive and coming at you from left field.

For those who are wondering, "Tofe, that's all well and good, but how do I know your methods are true?" Well, I've been fortunate enough to be connected with mental health professionals along the way who have shaped my beliefs on healthy striving, resilience, and personal growth. I've drawn from the wisdom of psychologists, researchers, behavioral scientists, authors, and influential thinkers who have helped me to better understand myself and my process, and to make sense of my journey. I've learned about the psychology of fear and trust, the neurobiology of emotion, and the importance of human connection. I've spent countless hours integrating scientific findings from neurobiology, psychology, and philosophy with my own life experiences. In the chapters that follow, I apply this wisdom to my own journey, and my hope is that these ideas will help you to better know your own path.

Where I've lived through a raw experience and been an advocate on resilience testing in practical settings every day, I've attained evidence from the professionals to confirm the analytical and data side of things. I know this tested knowledge and experience I have had will validate 100 percent that my process works. These processes will work for you as well, and they will propel you out of those nasty rabbit holes and, better yet, push you beyond any limits you didn't think were possible.

It is vital that we don't limit our thinking. The goal is for you to become someone who previously thought something was *impossible*, but now you know you can turn that into a statement and life view that says, *"I'M* **POSSIBLE!"**

Here, you can focus on disrupting the everyday, conventional thinking. Where you want to quicken the process a little, I've come across several methods and mind hacks learned through the philosophies of the greats—or on my own—via endurance and by testing them myself. I can attest that they will definitely work for you, preventing you from becoming the bitch of your own brain.

Now, you may not have any inclination toward the topic of endurance or toward running more than 160 km at a time (and keep in mind that 16 km is about 10 mi.). You can, however, most definitely learn from someone who deliberately puts his body through stressful situations every day to overcome adversity and unlock untapped sections of the mind.

There will be a time in your life when you face a crisis; it could be a recession, a death in the family, a bad business deal, or even a life-threatening situation. How will you deal with these high-stress moments? That's where this book will be your toolkit, mentally guiding you out of these adversarial and dismal situations.

Before I continue, I want to be clear about what I do. I'm a thought leader on resilience, not on hacking the body to get you the set of abs you've always wanted. I'm here so you have the mental artillery to hold yourself together in case of a traumatic crisis. If you want the perfect body, I'm not your guy for that. When everyone is focused on having a six-pack body they forget that having a six-pack mind is more important.

At the end of the day, **EVERYONE HAS A PLAN UNTIL**

SHIT HITS THE FAN, so treat this as if it's your "Practical Resilience Bible," so your planning is in place in advance of any crisis.

Enjoy!

Tofe Evans
Resilience Thought Leader

CHAPTER 1

REACHING YOUR BREAKING POINT

"I think I'm ready to end this. The head smog that's built up like an overflowing blender is at an all-time high, I'm scared for my life. I have one thing on my mind and one thing only—the summoning of an overdose has me all-ears; it's got my full undivided attention." —July 19, 2014

When I think of greatness, I think breaking world records, winning gold medals, and even racing a shark. Some look at Michael Phelps as a world-class swimmer, but I see him as a childhood hero. I still remember the last four or five Olympics, watching this specimen dominate beyond the pool, taking over the Olympics and becoming the go-to dude to watch. His composure in high-stress moments was mesmerizing. It grew on me, a desire to be like him one day.

While Phelps had such an impact on me, so did another Olympic swimmer—Ian Thorpe. I adored this guy growing up. He may have been the youngest guy in the lane, but there was this hope to see a kid's strong determination to win turn to fruition. Every night he was on TV, racing in the Sydney Olympics, I'd be cheering at the top of my lungs hoping he'd hear me and move quicker to bring home multiple gold medals for Australia. That he did!

Where these two swimming legends have lived through amazing herculean careers, they've both also had their mental battles and struggled with depression for years. Phelps took a break after the London 2012 games, but he fell into a deep enough rabbit hole that his rambunctious party antics, mixed with his depression, queued him to get some help really quick. As for Thorpe, depression stuck with him throughout his high school years, crippling him mentally and causing him to hide his sexuality until 2014, when he came out as gay. Drowning his sorrows in copious amounts of alcohol was his way of dealing with it and his only way of getting sleep.

It doesn't make sense that these two guys who seemed to have it great had been living in such psychological misery, without anyone knowing.

Hearing two of my favorite athletes come out and speak about their mental health struggles was a vivid moment.

Seeing how these super humans were suffering, and no one had known, made me realize this was a massive problem. No one should be experiencing this.

It turns out, they're just human beings too. They demonstrate that mental health is a real thing and a major world issue. In Australia alone there are everyday people, both young and old, struggling with anxiety and depression, and the number of struggling people is rising by the minute. Nine times out of ten, we end up bottling our emotions and resorting to substances we believe are the only answer. It happens every day to ordinary people.

The thing is, there's another way out.

But first, let me tell you about my friend, Jake Malby, who was one of the victims experiencing chronic mental health problems. Throughout his high school days he dealt with heavy anxiety issues; but, because he appeared to be such a normal kid at school, no one knew he was suffering. For many, it's as if there's a mask that hides everything and makes things look fine. In actuality, those inner struggles are an active volcano ready to erupt any minute. In these cases, the red-hot lava might be closer to overflowing than you think, resulting in a chaotic mess.

Frustrated with what he was experiencing, Jake put all the blame on himself. Living with a load of invisible weight on his shoulders only made matters worse. It was a burden that shouldn't have been there at all. Anyone in such a sticky situation would be thinking, "What did I do to deserve this?" Some battle it forever, and some get to a point where they can't handle it anymore. This brings me to my own personal story.

FROM THE RIGHT TRACK TO OFF-ROADING

You know that feeling when things are going right and life is good, but the next minute, you're off-road and wondering how you go there? Suddenly, you're a train wreck. I've been there myself, and it wasn't pretty.

I was a generally happy person until a series of events—relationships, work, business, family, etc.—happened in 2014 that caused me to enter a negative and melancholy state. I stopped looking after myself, both mentally and physically. I turned into an entirely different person. I went from a kid who was joyful and fun-loving to that depressed, resentful burden who attracted nobody.

At that current state of rock-bottom, I'd resorted to a chemical bias—a heavy intake of hard drugs and alcohol. Life felt so shitty I needed reassurance. I relied on substances that I hoped would make me better, but in fact, I wasn't making my situation preventable, only worse. Then the self-harm began, which seemed to be a great idea at the time, because the chemical dependency wasn't working as well as I had expected.

This was all happening when I was travelling the world—a time you'd think I'd cherish the most and would've had no troubles whatsoever. Don't get me wrong, I had such an amazing time and experienced everything from dog-sledding in the snow, to being in the town that won a Super Bowl, to road-tripping the entire east coast of America. Those memories have so much sentimental value. I was approximately six months into 2014 when a string of set-backs started happening. Then, before I knew it, I was going off the rails.

Everything became a constant worry, to the point that something as remarkably miniscule as a pen running out of ink suddenly became a struggle I could hardly deal with. Brain fog and black clouds seemed to circle around in my head creating the next Hurricane Katrina. It felt like a whirlwind of emotions with no let up and no clarity. What happens when you have far too much on your mind? You tend to have trouble sleeping.

At one point, while I was traveling throughout the US, I stayed with a friend in Dallas, Texas. I was scheduled for a flight to Chicago the next day. Needing someone to talk to, I explained to my friend how I was having trouble sleeping due to various stressful issues in my life. I told her that I needed sleeping pills to forcefully knock me out just so I could get some sleep. I also mentioned that I took a few other meds to reduce my anxiety. But here's the kicker—my friend who gave me advice also lent me the meds. The situation wasn't her fault; she was just trying to help this restless mess who was seeking guidance and some sort of light at the end of the tunnel.

At first, it was wonderful. I could finally sleep. But the pills knocked me out for twelve hours at a time from deprivation. I would wake up feeling so groggy that I had no idea even what year it was. It would take another half day to rejuvenate, and by then, the day was over and the cycle would repeat. The same thing was true for the anxiety meds. The constant worry would subside enough for me to articulate what was happening each day; however, I was still far from happy. I stopped taking the sleeping medication once I ran out of the batch my friend had given me, though there were plenty of anxiety pills remaining. There were a couple kinds to pick from, depending on whether I was in real trouble or just needed to feel comfortable.

Now, not only is it a really bad idea to be consuming other people's prescription drugs, but mixing them with hard drugs and alcohol could cause a reaction that would be the end of everything. Weeks had gone by and my "worry meter" was still on high "Code Red." I was ready to implode at any minute. With this becoming my constant feeling, I was getting used to the intensity and just assumed it was meant to be that way.

It was at that moment my friends started getting worried. They constantly told me to see a doctor, so I began thinking, "Wow, have I really gotten to this point in life? I thought these kinds of problems only happened to rock stars!" It made sense though. I was experiencing such misery; it was hard to smile, and everything was dark. I literally couldn't see light in the day, just blackened skies.

By now, I was travelling through Toronto, Canada. It was a place I'd never visited and I was feeling more alone than ever—unable to speak out for help because, well, I'm a guy and we're not meant to divulge and express feelings, right? Feeling sick and tired of "feeling sick and tired," I eventually gathered the courage to see a doctor. He warned me of the circumstances and dangers of using prescription medication that wasn't mine. His solution? Get off those and use the ones you should be on." Oh, what a relief! I was using the wrong meds.

Here's the thing with pills, whether they're for medicinal or recreational purposes, all those chemicals bring through a rush of dopamine and can be followed by an array of symptoms. Those symptoms didn't help the situation because they introduced a new plethora of problems.

For me, they reduced my anxiety, but they were doing the opposite for my depression.

Having both anxiety and depression working together is a nightmare beyond belief. Anxiety is when you can't stop thinking about everything, and depression is when you don't care about anything at all. And if both of these are acting at once, it will result in an endless mental battle of tug of war. It's as if you're at school camp playing tug of war by yourself against two strong kids. You can't win.

Travelling the world was far from exciting at this point. I came to the realization that feeling this alone and isolated could be an indicator that it was time for me to fly back home and get my shit together. So, I did exactly that and instantly missed what I'd left behind—from the brutal summer days to the smell of salty air at the beach. However, my meds had run out from my last batch in Canada, so it made sense to get more. I saw my general physician who instantly noticed my unhappy emotional state. He insisted on trying a brand of drug that could ease both anxiety and depression, "though symptoms apply."

We always hear those three words, "though symptoms apply," and automatically assume it will be alright because everyone is different. Though, when you're dealing with someone's head—how they think, their cognitive functions, their mental and emotional engines—there's a chance those symptoms are making things worse, rather than bearable.

Now, I'm not telling you to quit a medication if you're already on it. I'm speaking from my own personal experience, and these new meds did nothing but cause me more grief. Some people in this world have a chemical or hormonal imbalance that conflicts with a prescribed antidote. But, understand, I'm not disparaging the situation for those who need to take a medication. Like I said, I'm just speaking from my own experience.

However, for those having trouble dealing with a crisis and feel it's necessary to see the doctor to try a medication for the first time, just realize that, as you continue to read this book, there is a safer way out. Medication is designed to be a stabilizer, but as soon as they become abused, they can backfire and make matters worse.

A week passed with this new hopeful solution, and what was originally meant to be a band-aid became keys to an uncontrollable moving car headed for the edge of a cliff. That's where my mind was headed. I was relapsing.

I'll admit, I reached a juncture in life, an era where it all seemed too much. While an overdose did make its way around, it didn't finish the job. It didn't end there. There were many times I Googled "ways to kill myself." Puddles of tears would cover the screen as I'd wander into sites with notices warning, "Not recommended to click on these links." All hope was gone and I became so lost in my thoughts that if I didn't do something quick enough, the negative rabbit hole I was digging would soon lead to my grave.

That thought was enough impetus to make me realize no one should be feeling like this. So, as a last resort, I listened to my intuition and gathered the courage to quit the pills and every other coping mechanism I had succumbed to. I needed to figure out, "Why am I not happy?" I had to reach out to save this restless soul. This became the start of my own personal rehabilitation process.

It may have taken a couple years, but I had a gut feeling that hope was my foundation, and the process was quicker than I had expected.

THE TURNING POINT

A lightbulb went on and a new focus arose: getting some sort of movement into the body, shifting those idolized, worried thoughts into sweat and endorphins. Soon after, and with the extensive repetition of not knowing what the hell I was doing, I was able to shift my perspective from past-focused living to present-focused living. I was actually living in the "now."

Children live and engage in present-focused living, like playing sports with their friends, while most of us are actually living in the past. Somewhere between childhood and adulthood, we disconnect from what feels right and what resonates with us, and we start going down that path of what we think we should be doing. It's crucial that we engage in more present-focus, giving our full, undivided attention to keeping us grounded. Too many of us have our minds wandering around other planets.

Those who are fixated on the past need to be fixated on the path, instead.

—TOFE EVANS

AWAY FROM PAST FIXATION AND TOWARD THE PATH

You cannot change the past, therefore, do not even bother investing time into those thoughts of "What if?" or "I wish I could change…" because you're wasting your time.

Where therapy is known to some as seeing a psychiatrist, there's an alternative method that is more effective and practical. The more I study this, the more I notice this emerging method actually helps self-regulate the mind away from clutter through present-focused living. And that method is using running as therapy. Other people use other sports, or knitting, or even writing to express their feelings through different channels.

Running a race is identical to life's adversity—feelings of hopelessness, excitement, adrenaline, and pushing through pain. Life is an ultramarathon. It doesn't matter what the distance is, everyone has their own ultramarathon to work through, whether it is getting off the couch or actually running a 250 km event.

There's definitely an energy or presence of some sort that pushes you in the same direction, similar to how life events have you come face-to-face with reality. We dig deep to fully wrestle with our incredulous self-doubts and thoughts—that's what's stopping us. Where things seem incredibly tough, we must remember we're in this together, slowly building a warrior mindset within, and it becomes a team effort more than anything else. I feel this everyday, especially through the connection of a running community.

What are the three profound mindsets that running has taught me, you might ask?

1. Running has taught me to complain less.
2. Running has made me grateful for what I have.
3. Running has taught me how to push through adversity.

I don't care if these sound cheesy to you—this is exactly what running has done for me.

Here's why:

1. RUNNING HAS TAUGHT ME TO COMPLAIN LESS, MUCH LESS.

In the very large handful of events I've completed, as well as the mandatory physical training each week, I've managed to put my body through a strenuous amount of exercise. I've clocked thousands of kilometers and have competed in races that would seem insane or crazy to some. But after all the training, and even better, finishing these races, I just know that it was the toughest thing I could achieve. As soon as the thought "this is too hard" comes into my mind, I know that any problem I encounter is near nothing because I've legitimately dealt with tougher times. On the days when things aren't quite right, or when I don't train, an odd feeling may overcome me, things might get to me, but then I just put my thoughts in perspective. I know that I've put my body through races that last longer than twelve hours, and I think about those who are amputees who choose to run on a prosthetic leg. So, I don't complain, because there is ALWAYS someone with more challenges than me.

2. RUNNING HAS MADE ME GRATEFUL FOR WHAT I HAVE.

When I'm facing a mental wall, I might be at the stage where I just want to crawl in a bed because I've been on my feet for twenty-plus hours, or want to eat because I've burnt more calories than my weekly calorie intake, or my Camelbak has run out of water and I'm feeling dehydrated. Completing a massive run instantly gives you feelings of relief; and by the end, you're just happy to have food, shelter, water, and people around you. At that moment, I don't care what kind of car I own, I just need it to get me to a bed—and I couldn't care less what bed I have or about anything materialistic because I'm just grateful for the fundamentals in life. Finishing a race has me so physically worn out that the basics are all I need.

It has also rewired my brain to avoid purchasing things that rust, rot, and depreciate, and it has sparked an investor mindset of thinking long term.

3. RUNNING HAS TAUGHT ME HOW TO PUSH THROUGH ADVERSITY.

One of the greatest things ever said was by Will Smith. During a speech to a group of school kids, Will said that the two most important things in life were reading and running. I won't go into too much detail with the reading, but he said running is important because it teaches you how to push through a race even when it gets tough and when your lungs feel like they're out of air. He told the kids to apply this mentality to their everyday problems and they'll have more control in their life.

Having run multiple ultramarathons, there were often moments when I'd reach a mental wall and find myself at the lowest of lows. Those moments usually come when you've been running for so many hours that the GPS watch has died, or the "tenth-wind" has diminished and doubt is flooding back in, all intertwined with surreptitious injury. During ultramarathons, the body just wants to give up, but I know I need to push on. It's hard to control the mind and get back on track, but once it's back, the body will be too. As Will Smith said, "When you're running, there's a little person that talks to you and says, 'Oh I'm tired. My lung's about to pop I'm so hurt. I'm so tired. There's no way I can possibly continue.' And you want to quit, right? f you learn how to defeat that person when you're running you will learn how to not quit when things get hard in your life."

This mindset has been the most profound of all three. Who would've thought running would be the greatest philosopher and teacher I could have asked for? It gives me goosebumps to think about it, knowing endurance and gratitude were the antidote that saved me from taking my own life.

CHAPTER 2

PHILOSOPHY: BEING IN CONTROL OF YOUR THINKING

"Using those muscles to raise my mouth into what's known as a smile is becoming harder each day. What's the point? No point faking emotion when something feels so missing. This is heartbreaking, I'm usually known as a person who is ceaselessly smiling. Constant manic rushes of despair are coming in and out of me like a bad spirit toying with a possessed being. Wow, am I really to this point in life? I literally can't see light in the day, just blackened skies." —July 27, 2014

Seven and a half billion. That is the number of people wandering this earth right now. By the time this is published, it may be closer to eight billion, each on their own path discovering a new journey. Some might be wondering how they'll get there, while others already know their path. Seven and a half billion different people with seven and a half billion different brains and unique styles of thinking. As young children developing into adults, we aim to have our shit together by the time we're fully grown. A package of evolving beings comes with convictions, validating the thought process of learning what's right or wrong.

Some things we're entirely certain about, making a decision simpler. Then there's the uncertainty of everything else, resulting in a double-edged sword—exciting yet provocative, as we have no clue how to deal with the situation. So, as humans, we may attempt to process what's going on in our heads. We foresee the clear vision of perceived greatness and success, but negative thoughts may arise, triggering emotional and traumatic life experiences, which cause the thought process to go haywire. We find ourselves missing the vision completely with our focus shifted back on the past and our previous mistakes. This comes back to what I said earlier. We tend to be fixated on the past instead of the path.

This is the survival part of our brains being activated, also known as the reptilian, ancestral, primal brain. It's the ten-thousand-plus-year-old DNA still carried in our thoughts. We're hardwired to protect ourselves and to survive fear. Our brains have not changed that much since our early ancestral days. When you were ostracized from the tribe thousands of years ago, you were thrown out into the open, scared for your life by the threat of lions and tigers. Well, you know that feeling when you've been betrayed by a friend or family member or alienated from your social circles for whatever reason? It's a completely identical feeling to the tribe kicking you out—we still feel as if a lion or tiger is after us.

It's the same thing as when we hunted for food and resources as hunter-gatherers. There was a likely chance we might not eat for days on end; so, if we got the chance to eat, we'd seize the moment to get that nourishment, because it might be the last time to do so. Nowadays, we have access to food and extensive resources, and sometimes we tend to overeat and indulge. There's still that primal trigger in the brain wondering whether we'll ever have the chance to eat again. We've literally gone from one extreme of malnutrition to the other—from starvation to obesity.

As a species, we've developed and conquered more than we ever imagined; what we've accomplished is quite impressive. Polio doesn't exist anymore, and our phones are more advanced than the spaceships that put mankind on the moon back in '69. We may have advanced technologically as a nation, but our state of *fear* has changed only by a fraction.

Through our negative thoughts that are provoked by emotional triggers, we dig ourselves into a rabbit hole, with hours if not decades of time invested into these agonizing and wasted moments. We are so certain that what's going on in our heads is 110 percent correct that we become resentful, holding onto black-and-white mentalities, and we're cynical of anything unfamiliar to what the psyche can perceive. It's as if the story we're narrating subconsciously is validation for our fixed beliefs, which include our views and convictions—in fancier terminology, the paradigm we live in.

The greatest and renowned leaders in history, some of whom weren't perceived as great at first, had strong convictions. Nelson Mandela, for example, in his rebellion, was shunned and imprisoned in South Africa for twenty-seven years for protesting his rights. There, he maintained his composure and his beliefs. Years after his release, he became one of the most prolific and inspiring icons to have stood the test of time.

Then there are leaders whose convictions have done more destruction than imaginable. Adolf Hitler and Joseph Stalin are prime examples. I got won't go into too much detail, but their egos got so far out of control and caused such devastation that it was more of a celebration than a loss when they died.

BETTERING OUR THOUGHT PROCESS

How do we better our thought process? We change our understanding. This is the moment we recognize that we can't be black-and-white cynics. That's a paradigm shift in itself. It comes down to the quote from American Politician, Donald Rumsfeld:

"There are known-knowns; there are things we know we know. We also know there are known-unknowns; that is to say we know there are some things we do not know. But there are also unknown-unknowns—the ones we don't know we don't know."

Going from my own life's example, in 2014, I was mentally sick and inept during my struggle. I thought I knew what was happening, but I never gave many other options a chance—what I now know were unknown-unknowns back then. Here's a then and now breakdown of my convictions.

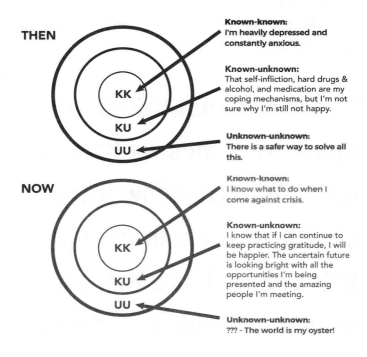

THEN

Known-known:
I'm heavily depressed and constantly anxious.

Known-unknown:
That self-infliction, hard drugs & alcohol, and medication are my coping mechanisms, but I'm not sure why I'm still not happy.

Unknown-unknown:
There is a safer way to solve all this.

NOW

Known-known:
I know what to do when I come against crisis.

Known-unknown:
I know that if I can continue to keep practicing gratitude, I will be happier. The uncertain future is looking bright with all the opportunities I'm being presented and the amazing people I'm meeting.

Unknown-unknown:
??? - The world is my oyster!

Some of you fall under the THEN, the first set of KK/KU/ UU, and that's okay! Just realize that this book is your Practical Resilience Bible. It'll get you out of that state so your new thoughts become the NOW set of KK/KU/UU, which will supersede any negative mindset that's holding you back from living the life you want!

I know how you feel if you're experiencing that first set of KK/

KU/UU—you're lost beyond words and feel more alone than ever. Even though you may be surrounded by people trying to help you, there's still a sense of loneliness, and reaching out to friends, family, or a specialist is the last thing you want to do. You feel like a burden, knowing they have their own problems to deal with; essentially, we are holding ourselves back and these emotions are suppressing our vulnerability. We've closed off who we are and we're no longer able to be 100 percent of the human beings we were meant to be.

If you are in this situation, please reach out. It takes courage to ask for help and let someone see your vulnerable state. How many of us are shunned, put down, or shamed if we go against social pressures and divulge our feelings? Especially for us guys? We get called a pussy or weak if we need to cry or choose not to drink beer. It's funny how testosterone can take over the best of us.

Holding onto emotional baggage will magnify the problem over time. Wouldn't you rather invest that wasted energy in bigger and better things? That's why I'm glad to open up about my challenging experiences; not only does it take the weight off my shoulders, but others who are struggling may resonate with my story and confront their own demons. It may give them the permission they need to open up and speak out, to get it off their chest, and, more importantly, to move forward. I hope to be the vehicle that brings reassurance to others.

OUR STORY CAN HEAL OTHERS

When we open up, it heals us and allows others to do the same. If you hold onto a bottle of water that weighs about a half of a kilogram (or about 1 lb.), it's not a big deal; but, when you continue to hold onto it for twenty-four hours, then it'll begin to feel like 100 kg, even though it hasn't changed in material properties over that time. Now, apply this analogy to our thoughts. Our mind is like an attic—it can only hold so much, and any irrelevant and burdening thoughts will magnify into a 300 kg weight. Then, in no time, 300 kg magnifies to 600 kg, and so on. It's incredibly liberating when you can open up and get something off your chest. You feel an instant sense of relief and you find you have more room for better thoughts.

Opening up for the first time is never easy. It took me years to tell my story. I cared too much about what others would think of me. Now, I realize that anyone can have a messed-up past. I'm not the only one who's going through this, so who's to judge?

HOW CAN I BE MORE VULNERABLE?

Here are three practical ways to increase your receptivity; like anything new, these may feel uncomfortable or unnatural at first. But keep at it.

1. If you feel the need to cry or open up to someone, do

it as often as you can so those emotions get out of your system.

2. Become more empathetic. Listening to others and being on the same level will build a stronger relationship, helping all sides understand each other.

3. Reach out if you're battling depression, anxiety, PTSD, or any type of unbearable adversity. If you are afraid to talk to friends and family, call the crisis support phone number in your city. They won't judge you about your situation. Their team will understand and help you, because it's actually their job.

YOU ARE GREAT AND FAR FROM WORTHLESS!

You may have a messed up past or no self-esteem right now, but that's okay. All the greats went through a period like this in their life somewhere along their journey. After researching and obsessively studying the greats who have stood the test of time, every single one of them has had a life trajectory filled with pain! Where they stand out from the rest of the crowd is in their discipline to keep going when nobody's watching.

Below is a table of history's well-known iconic greats who battled their inner demons and were able to achieve a level of success and greatness as a result of the process.

ICON	INNER DEMONS	WHAT THEY'RE KNOWN FOR
Arnold Schwarzenegger	Being told he wouldn't make it in acting because no one could pronounce his last name, and because he had a strong German accent.	Eight-time award winner of Mr. Olympia contest, A-grade actor, and former governor of California
Conor McGregor	Growing up homeless and resourceless	Two-time UFC Division Champion
Elon Musk	Incredibly high levels of stress while building three companies simultaneously	The man who will put people on Mars
Eminem	Years of family struggles	Hall of Fame rapper
Joe De Sena	Became physically unfit during his career on Wall Street	Founder of Spartan Race
Michael Jordan	His father was murdered after his first three-peat win/first retirement	Six-time NBA Champion and the GOAT of basketball
Michael Phelps	Depression after competing four times in the Olympics	He competed for a fifth time in the Olympics and won four more gold medals. In total, he won twenty-three Olympic gold medals and is a world record holder.
Nelson Mandela	Spent twenty-seven years in prison protesting his rights	South Africa's first black president and a top influential icon in history.
Oprah Winfrey	Was told she'd never be a great fit for television and was sexually abused growing up	Most influential female TV personality

This is blank so YOU can write your name here and note what troubles you're experiencing and what you'll be known for!

When we're on this path, we can either attract those who want greatness or those who settle for mediocrity. The ones who strive for greatness usually never complain, even when their stress levels are high. It's important to focus only on those things you can control. It's up to you to decide whether what you're going through is a tiny inconvenience or setback, or a huge problem that will impact your life's outcome.

Furthermore, there are three types of issues in this world that we can or can't solve. The following table lists several examples.

DIRECT: THINGS WE CAN FIX	INDIRECT: THINGS WE CAN'T FIX ON OUR OWN; SHAREABLE	UNCONTROLLABLE: THINGS WE CAN'T FIX AND ARE OUT OF OUR CONTROL
Weight control	Relationships	Natural disasters/
Financial	Mental health stigma	weather
independence	Global poverty	Road traffic
Depression	Petition to get an	Death
Managing character	event to your city	Silencing thoughts
traits (gratitude)	Fundraising for	Reversing time/
How much rest you	treatment	the past
get each night	Raising capital for	Petrol prices
First-world problems	the next stage of	Other people's
	your business	opinions

You might have something on your mind, and knowing which category it's in can help determine how you can respond. Is the problem listed in a specific category in the preceding table? If the problem is in the uncontrollable column, there's no point wasting your energy trying to find a solution.

Are you a complainer, or do you try to solve problems as they arise in your life?

NO FUCKING COMPLAINING

Unfortunately, too many people in the world today have a tendency to complain about the wrong things, like first-world problems. Even when you feel like complaining and letting everyone around you know what's on your mind, maybe you should think first and quietly decide how you could help solve the challenge you're facing. Otherwise, you'll attract other people who live their life complaining to everyone.

In the past, I've beaten myself up by worrying about how I reacted in a certain relationship. My increasing focus on the outcome only served to make me lose my self-confidence and create turmoil in my brain. Instead of fixating on the past, the solution was to fixate on the path.

A pivotal moment in my life occurred when I vowed to not complain about the wrong things. After working an exhausting eleven-hour day, I was mentally gearing up for my first 100 km ultramarathon race; it was the longest race I'd ever competed in. The race was scheduled to begin at 6:30 p.m., which meant I'd be running during the night, when normally I'd be asleep. I calculated that the race would take me about 12.5 hours to complete, and I had to focus on my path and get rid of all negative thoughts of fatigue during the run.

As I ran, I saw several homeless people sleeping under a bridge. My first thoughts were, "Damn, that looks comfortable." When I began thinking about how those homeless people looked while all curled up, it made me grateful that I wasn't homeless and that I had a bed to sleep in. More than that, I had a job, food, shelter, and water. I really had nothing to complain about, especially while running an ultramarathon. That sight kept me grounded. I knew that after running such a strenuous race, I was usually too wrecked to give a shit about what material items I owned. As long as I had a bed to crash in and some grub to restore those lost calories afterward, that was really all that mattered.

My intention is not to offend anyone but I've observed that, in today's society, we have soldiers with PTSD and African kids in developing third-world countries who are so grateful for what they have. Compare that to most "average" people today who think they have it tough because their Wi-Fi doesn't reach the other side of the house.

First of all, complaining adds no value to this world. Secondly, it attracts other complainers, and then they become your circle of influence. Research shows that people who complain a lot on their Facebook page are usually the ones who get unfollowed and unfriended the most. It comes down to Newton's third law of motion—every action has an opposite or equal reaction.

We all go through bad days and face challenges in our life, but that doesn't mean we have to post our exact thoughts on social media sites. In Eric Dezenhall's book, *Glass Jaw*, he states that if you're going through some adversarial moments in your life, it's best if you don't post anything about it on social media sites. He reasons that your negativity will not be helpful to anyone and it can get you in more trouble in the future by posting something you might later regret. What's more important is how you handle those problems.

Honestly? No one gives a shit about how much your boyfriend isn't paying attention to you, or how your boss won't give you that raise. There isn't a person alive who doesn't have their own problems to deal with every day. In fact, it says more about your integrity if you remain cool under pressure. If your issue doesn't require serious help from a health professional, then you should contact a friend and talk about what's bothering you over the phone or in person. That's a much smarter decision than to post your biased and negative thoughts on social media sites.

If your issues concern your financial situation, instead of whining about how you don't have enough money, then you might want to consider working harder, getting a second job, or talking to someone who can help you reduce your debt. Maybe you continue to spend money instead of "doing without" for a while. Even if you're working a shit-ton of hours this week, don't be tempted to complain to strangers on Facebook about how many hours you've had to work lately. They won't be sympathetic with you and your negative words won't affect them.

Or maybe you're someone who complains about "how fat you are." As I said earlier, if you make a plan and follow through with it, you will achieve the results you want. For example, if you cut out all processed foods and refined sugars, and make it a priority to exercise every day, then you'll start realizing new levels of weight loss.

But none of this advice is effective until you make a purposeful mental shift to think about what you want as your long-term results. Make sure every decision you make will have a positive effect on your life, or else, don't do it. The same reasoning applies to anything that involves money. Just remember, it's not the price that matters, it's the value it brings to your life.

For example, if you buy a three-dollar burger at McDonald's, it might not jeopardize your chances of becoming healthier, but it's the worst three dollars you can spend. Why? It will be gone in five minutes, and all you're doing is making McDonald's richer. Instead, why not invest that three dollars in a healthier food choice? Or better yet, take that money and invest in a fitness program that will give you a healthier lifestyle.

For me, I get frustrated when I hear people complain about things they can't control. These things include gasoline prices, the stock exchange, and even "how things aren't as great as they used to be." It's obvious the gas giants are the ones to blame for the escalating prices, but if you're not going to do something about it, then keep your mouth shut. If you really care, think of something you can do to save on your gas expenses. Maybe you could buy an electric car or design an app that allows you to collaborate with the gas giants to offer discounted gas. I don't care how you solve this problem, just don't complain about the high price of gas if you're not going to do anything about it.

If you're someone who tends to dwell on the past and you keep reminding everyone about how life was thirty years ago, then you're living in your own world, man. Just know that even though war and corruption are still in the news, we are living in the most advanced, easily-accessed, creative times. Learn to embrace what's around you. Then you might enjoy these modern times a little more.

In my opinion, the one thing you should reflect on about your past is seeing how far you've come. If you're at the lowest point of your life right now, then beginning with today—don't think about your life circumstances until one or two years from now. And don't complain during this growth process.

The same is true about politics. If you don't like or agree with what the current politician is doing, then join your local party and get involved with their goals. Maybe if the people in this world spent less time complaining about useless topics, we would be living in a much more innovative place.

We tend to blame the media for the level of news that's reported these days. As an observer, I don't understand why many parents encourage their kids to watch the news. All that's talked about, for the most part, is death, crime, and negativity. It's obvious these topics are appealing to the human brain and those who thrive on the news 24/7, but it doesn't do any good because it doesn't embrace creativity. Instead, it's just nitpicky and it affects people's outlook. It doesn't matter whether you're eighteen or eighty and you're reading this. Just do what you can and don't complain!

None of us are entitled to anything. The world owes you nothing. Just the fact that you've been born and have the chance to live should be enough impetus for you to realize you can make anything happen. If you

want something, work hard for it. Don't try to convince yourself that you actually deserve it. Don't wish for what you want and think you'll get it by gambling on the lottery every weekend.

The important things are locked in the lexicon while the useless ones are removed. Yay, more room for creativity! Here's the thing about creativity, the less of it you have, the faster you'll move away from your dreams and aspirations. It's inversely proportional. If you feel as if you have no creativity, then hire someone to brainstorm with you and get some new ideas.

I love being around young people and kids, because they're so playful and creative. Give a child a container of Lego blocks and we're going to the moon, man! Why do we lose our creativity when we get older when we were so full of it at a much younger age? I don't want to blame the current school system, but their style of teaching isn't working. They cram all this information into your head so you hate it.

I thoroughly disliked history and poetry when I was in school. Mostly, I didn't like the school's teaching methods. But now that I'm older, I love these subjects. I needed to alter my mindset. When I simply stopped thinking in black-and-white, I became a lot more curious. In my opinion, schools should be teaching character traits as a mandatory subject. Curiosity is key to an active and healthy brain, so why not make this a high priority regardless of age?

GET CURIOUS AND ASK MORE QUESTIONS

When you start thinking and ask more "Why?" questions, it's likely your creativity will increase. When you ask more questions and become a little more curious, it's as if your brain begins tapping into unknown areas that will increase your fascination with everything. Who knows, you could be only a couple questions away from discovering a new-found love in an area you hadn't thought about before. That's what happened to me. It's how I discovered my adoration for endurance and my obsession with resilience.

During your formative years at school, you were asked, "What do you want to be when you grow up?" Often, the answers were astounding. "Spaceman," or, "I want to save the world" were normal responses; but, as the child grew up and the years passed by, the answers changed drastically. Suddenly, those children were faced with having to work in dead-end jobs to pay the bills.

That's not livin', Barry!

Some kids went to a local college or university in another city, and their desired occupation required years of mental struggle to get that piece of paper stating that they were now qualified. But that isn't really living either, is it? Besides aspiring to be a lawyer or doctor, you can actually work at any job without a tertiary education. When the opportunity is presented to you, just say yes, and then figure out how to do the job along the way.

"You jump off a cliff and you assemble an airplane on the way down."

—REID HOFFMAN

I know talking about Donald Trump is a controversial and touchy topic, but the guy had no experience in politics, and then he managed to become the forty-fifth president of the United States. Whether he's intellectual enough to be a world leader is another topic.

I don't think universities and colleges are entirely a waste of time. If you want to be a scientist, doctor, or lawyer, then go to school for it. But if you want to be in business or you want to be a marketing guru, don't waste your time. Half the time, a lecturer who is teaching business skills has never started or sold a business before. However, although it's important to know the fundamentals, don't overpay for something that's undervalued. It would make more sense to spend your money on several mentors who know their shit better than anyone else, because they will cut your learning curve by years, if not decades.

I have never gone to university, but I collaborate with those who have their degrees. I have conducted research for impact and empowering reasons. To be known as that kid who pushed the boundaries and became part of research studies with some of the greatest minds out there, is to be a step closer to finding cures and long-sought-after answers. It's much more gratifying than getting a degree that may not get its full use.

I don't want to give the impression that I don't want to learn from universities, and I don't want to belittle those who are currently studying, but there is a lesson here. It's the importance of learning something new. I'm constantly reading non-fiction books, and I often take on MOOCs (massive open online courses) so I can take almost any course from several universities and even Ivy League colleges, for free! Even YouTube has free courses from Yale. So, that's a little life hack for you. It doesn't matter how you're assimilating the learning. At the end of the day—whether you're learning from an online university, from free MOOCs, or from mentors—time is your most valuable commodity. It's up to you to learn the most you can about a topic that interests you, so you can substantially cut your learning curve.

I remember taking free financial MOOCs offered by Stanford University, a prolific American tertiary university, even though I was living in Australia. Acquiring the knowledge and not getting the degree seems like a win-win to me. But if the certificate is something you'd like to add to your resume, you can obtain it from a MOOC if you want!

Going back to the school system as mentioned earlier, there are educational centers such as Montessori schools that embrace a different learning style method for students. They are the ones who are looking after this hypo-creativity situation.

Fun fact: The Google founders, Larry Page and Sergey Brin, both attended Montessori schools.

TRAVEL AS MUCH AS POSSIBLE

Another creativity booster tip is to travel as much as you can, especially to third-world countries and places where culture sticks out like a dog's balls.

Why is travel important?

1. It'll make you appreciate what you have even before you get back home.
2. Your creativity will grow because seeing things done differently will make you start asking "Why?" a lot more. Exploring a new culture is an eye-opener.
3. Every city has its own personality and vibe. Why not see other cities to experience this and make new friends in other countries?

If you have a chance to visit Japan, go there and see everything you can. Besides its welcoming energy and very polite citizens, Japan is a country that operates so differently that it will make you wonder why they do things the way they do. There's no such thing as too much creativity!

Nepal is a place that will always be close to my heart not only because of its ingenuity, but because the locals treat you like family. Whether they're Sherpas, porters, or any Nepali, they will greet you with open arms. This is especially true since most of them aren't born with money or luxurious material items. You might be wondering how on earth they can be so happy living in such terrible conditions. The simple answer is because they've gone through all the hardships and adversity. They're grateful to have family and everything in full supply available to them. Since they possess only those items that really mean something to them, that's all they need.

It's an old saying that once you've walked a mile in another man's shoes, only then will you truly understand their life's perspective, and that leads to empathy. We live in a world of almost eight billion people, which means that everyone thinks differently and your own convictions might not be the same as someone else's.

When you're traveling through certain parts of the world, your patience could easily be tested. In extremely populated countries like India, where it's heavily congested, riding their metro train system can sometimes be frustrating if you're not used to it. I remember a time when I was on a metro ride back to where I was staying in Delhi, and the entire train was packed with people like a tin of sardines. Civilians were coming in and out at full force, but there was no point in losing my cool, because that's their normal way of life. One day when I was traveling around in a Rickshaw, every time we'd stop at a red light, a local would approach us and beg for money. It usually took me a few times of saying no before they moved on. But they were so persistent.

GROW INTO THE PERSON YOU ASPIRE TO BE

Your challenge is to do something every day that scares you. Embrace the uncomfortable. When you do something outside of your comfort zone, your heart rate increases, the amygdala (the fear center of your brain) freaks out, and you start questioning yourself. But this is where the magic happens. Trust me! You'll be so timid at first that you might even regret you took a chance. Perfect! That's the beginning of a habit. By the sixty-sixth day of stepping out of your comfort zone, you'll be an entirely new person!

If you're wondering why you should do this for sixty-six days, it's because that's the minimum amount of time it takes to create a new habit. You may think it's twenty-one days, but according to The University College London, recent studies have shown that twenty-one days are not enough to establish a new habit. You can read more about this through this link: http://www.ucl.ac.uk/news/news-articles/0908/09080401.

Although you might experience a shift in your activities around the twenty-one-day mark, sixty-six days is the minimum amount of time for a new habit to embed itself in your neurology.

Ironically, during my high school years, I hated the following three things:

1. Running
2. Writing
3. Public speaking

However, today, I enjoy all three of these things, and I'm quite passionate about them too!

I may not be the best writer, but I've learned that everyone has their own style. I need to be my true self at all times. Although I'd like to think that my writing is perfect, perfectionism can kill the project, and it's the other extreme leading to moving too slow.

So, I just tell myself, "Good enough is perfect." And anything I can improve on is room for innovation.

WHAT TO DO WHEN THINGS AREN'T GOING AS PLANNED?

This is inevitable in every big venture you undertake. The key is to adapt. The first rule is don't panic or freak out, but instead, think of an alternative. Remember, there are twenty-six letters in the alphabet. If plan A or B isn't working, you can still move on to plan C.

I've competed in many ultramarathons where I had to adapt to certain "Oh, shit" moments. Take for example something as minor as running with a new blister, popping it early, and taping the foot up, or to something a little more rambunctious like when I ran a 160 km trail race in the Nerang Forest. It had 6,000 m (19,700 ft.) of cumulative vert. I started the race at 7:00 a.m., and by 2:00 a.m. my body was beyond fatigued. All I had was a dimly lit headlamp and a steep trail in front of me. Instantly, my focus had to become more intense, because if I tripped, it would not be pretty. An hour later, my eyes were beginning to close, and I decided to take a four-minute sleep. I found a bush nearby and set an alarm on my watch, hoping that it would wake me up. I had no intention of sleeping through it and getting a DNF (did not finish). The idea worked and surprisingly, I felt much better even after 240 seconds of rest.

I'm not sure what your situation is right now. You could be having a fallout with a partner, you may have just lost your job, or you might be dealing with burnout. As I mentioned earlier, don't panic—adapt. Your survival brain may be freaking out, but be conscious of what's going on within you and around you. Think of an effective alternative to get you out of your current setback.

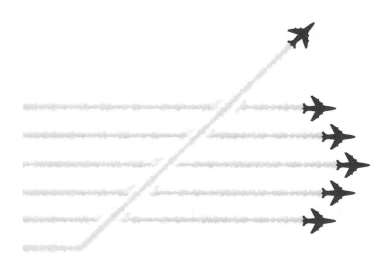

REMEMBER YOUR "WHY"

Taking on a new challenge is one thing, but staying persistent and pushing through until the end is something else. You will experience numerous times when it might seem too much for you to handle a certain situation. Or, you might just be having a bad day. During these moments, go back to the reason "why" you took up the challenge in the first place. This will keep you level-headed.

It's as if your thinking has reset itself and been recalibrated in such a way that you are now fully grounded and back on earth. Your mind may seem to wander out in space more than expected from time to time, but you're facing new challenges and overcoming new obstacles. Your brain is a brilliant self-accountability tool.

You might have purchased or received this book as a guide for learning how to attain a level of greatness. Or, this might be for you if you want a complete transformation that will drive you out of the troughs of sorrow. But maybe you have no idea what your "why" is. As you continue reading, you'll know your purpose by the time you get to the end of the book.

WHEN SOMEONE DOESN'T BELIEVE IN YOU

When someone tries to tell you that you can't do something, this is your chance to shut them up. There's no greater fuel than the words of those who didn't think you could do something. I didn't come from a running or sports-driven background. A lot of people in my life didn't think it was possible at the beginning of my rehabilitation journey that I could run extremely long distances.

When I took up endurance running in 2015, I was struggling with a bit of knee pain. The physio (at the time) said the issue had been *patella tendinitis*—the gel knee cap was easily moveable when it should be sturdy. I had done minimal running during the past two decades, and in the space of nine months I was at the 800 km mark. All the loading in my legs had been transferred to my knees, which resulted in my injury. During this phase of my life, I planned to run in a race scheduled for the next week. I had another one set for the following month. The physio's response, "Your knees are under quite the load. You probably shouldn't run too much because you don't have the legs for it."

"HOW DARE THAT BITCH SAY THAT!" I didn't say those words directly to her face, but I just smiled and nodded. The joke was on her though, because I ran so many more races successfully, in spite of her words cursing me. If anything, I should probably thank her for the extra fuel that ignited my whirlwind of a rebellious mind.

Realizing that running was working well for my health and

well-being, I was in no rush to give it up, so I never visited that physio again. The physios I see these days are particularly running- and endurance-based. Their responses for any injury prognosis are more reassuring, which is why I continue running these stupid long distances.

DEFYING THE ODDS

I was going through a time in my working life when I was getting sacked more than once. In fact, it became a great opportunity for me to start my own gig. So, I started a new business, several times. I had a plan, but because I was a one-man band, it meant I was doing everything. This is what's known as a solopreneur. I knew it was time to get out of my comfort zone and prepare to meet with prospective clients and turn them into customers. *Holy shit!* I had no fucking idea what I was doing at first. But in my mind, the fastest way to get in touch with other business owners was to attend as many networking meetings as possible. I literally signed up for every event available in the area. I drove an endless number of kilometers and spent hours meeting people. Positive things began happening when my new business plan became a habit.

Here's the thing with habits (and we'll talk more about rewiring your neural pathways to make fear your best friend in upcoming chapters): it all comes down to Isaac Newton's third law of motion—"Every action has an opposite and equal reaction." Meaning, that if you're not willing to put in the work, then don't bother complaining about how you're not seeing results.

If you don't put in the hours and hard work, then you won't get the results you want whether that'd be working on your business, health, happiness, or relationships.

What you put in is what you get out! It's as simple as that. Hey, it's simple, not easy!

A prime example of this is your health. In essence, if you don't eat well and do some sort of exercise on a regular basis every week, then you'll gain weight and have an unhealthy lifestyle.

Before you know it, you will start looking into fixing the issue at the worst possible moment. Chinese philosopher Lao Tzu says, "Do what's difficult today." That means don't wait until the problem has become worse than it should be.

This is a crucially important factor essential to everyone's life. Too many people ignore the following three scenarios before it's too late.

1. Seeing the psychologist to fix us mentally.
2. Trying a new diet to lose weight, because we've put on too many pounds.
3. Getting a loan to pay off the bills, because we have no savings account.

The problem with these solutions is you're taking action too fucking late.

Now, I'm no nutritionist or wealth strategist, but I can most definitely help you with the first item in the preceding list. It's important for you to continue reading this book over and over again so you're prepared for any crisis. You shouldn't have to see a psychologist and then be put on medical treatments when these issues can be fixed by just reading the methods described throughout this book.

Getting great results depends on the steps you take in your life. The first step is making the mental shift of enjoying what you have and being grateful. It allows you to get something done, and you'll be fine whenever you have to work those long days. I might not be a certified psychologist, but I'm a practitioner in the field working with these experts. Although I don't have the certificates or diplomas, my results are my experience. I've achieved the understanding, and I'm deliberately putting myself through stress to overcome all types of adversity. Tony Robbins, one of the world's famous life coaches, is also an expert on Neuro-Linguistic Programming (NLP) and he never went to university, yet he's the go-to guy for anything in life. This just proves that your results speak for your experience.

LET ME INTRODUCE PROFESSOR PETER REABURN

Professor Peter Reaburn is a dear friend of mine. Sports have been his lifelong passion. It started in 1965, when he was ten years old and joined the Southport Swimming Club on Queensland's Gold Coast. That's where he discovered the value of sports as well as the value of fitness and health, setting goals, overcoming adversity and hardship, and striving to achieve those goals. He also learned about the value of gaining lifelong friendships by sharing his sporting goals, along with the importance of overcoming adversity.

These values expanded as he moved through his teenage years and engaged in competitive rugby at school during the winter and while swimming and surf lifesaving on a national level during summer. Sports were so important to Peter that it became part of who he was. Sports helped define his self-concept and self-esteem. He soon became Peter Reaburn, the athlete, and Peter Reaburn, the person.

These same values helped him shape his career. Through university, he became a health and physical education teacher. He passed on his beloved passion and values to his primary and secondary school students. Then, he obtained his PhD in Sports Science, and he helped students become "disciples" of the code that we live and love by, which is sports.

Professor Reaburn now leads the exercise and sport science program at Bond University, a university where I've collaborated with instructors over the past year. The same values are being passed on to both his staff and students. Throughout his academic career, practicing what he preaches has been integral to his well-being.

Knowing Peter, he's never stopped competing, setting personal goals, and striving to achieve those goals. Overcoming adversity and making sacrifices to achieve those goals is also part of who he is. He went from setting the goal at age forty-five years to complete the Hawaii Kona Ironman Triathlon, which he first saw on TV in 1982 as a twenty-seven-year-old, to qualifying for Kona in 2005, where he won in his age group at the national Ironman triathlon championships. He came back to surf lifesaving in 2017, after thirty-eight years away, and won a gold medal at the national masters surf lifesaving championships.

Hard work, dedication, and a constant purpose got him there. The value set was locked in. Those values he learned as a ten-year-old are the same values he is true to today. Sports and the lessons he learned through striving to achieve his goals are the values embedded in his being.

INTEGRATION VS. BALANCE

With everything I'm juggling in my twenty-four-hour days, it's a fine art. Yes, I'm getting approximately six to seven hours of sleep a night, and it works for me because I can function totally fine throughout each day. Some of you need seven or eight hours to get you in the rhythm, and some of you have kids which adds another obstacle. Maybe you're one of those rare people who needs only four hours. It doesn't matter whether you have kids or you need nine hours of sleep. If you truly want something, you'll make it happen. When things seem out of balance, don't worry. Similar to how Arianna Huffington thinks about balance, I don't believe there's such a thing when it comes to our personal lives. Instead, we should focus on integration. I do believe there's a balance when we look at the world as a whole.

You won't have an exact balance when seeing friends, working on business, spending time with your family, and playing sports, so the most optimal way is by integrating those important life pillars into one mindset. For example, I love to travel, but after my experience traveling to get away from my everyday job and traveling for the sake of travel, I'd get the post-trip blues and return to a job I hated.

That's when I made a promise that if I travel, it's at least tied in with business, a charity project, or an endurance race. If I'm there for a reason, other than just to go on vacation, then I don't have to save up for a holiday and schedule time off from work.

Elon Musk says, "If you work 100 hours a week, then you will accomplish things 2.5 times faster than someone who works forty hours a week." As mentioned before, learn to love the grind! While everyone is sleeping at 9:00 p.m. or watching their favorite TV shows, I'm still up working to get things done.

If you're at a point in your life where you don't know what day it is, then something must be right. It's very confusing why people only love Fridays and weekends. I think that's pretty pathetic because more than half your life is spent at work. That's like saying you hate your job, which means you hate your life while you're working. So, to me, it makes no sense why people have this hardwired into their heads.

If you really do hate your job, then you should probably look into doing something on the side. By working on this as much as possible when you're not at work, you'll soon figure out how to monetize your business, which will give you a more stable income until you can think about quitting your day job. Then you can work on the business you enjoy, as long as you make sure you put in the hours and don't half-ass the process. It's possible for you to accomplish more than you could ever imagine.

CHAPTER 3

PRACTICAL RESILIENCE = ADVERSITY X MINDSET X GRATITUDE

"The doctor was right. I was struggling big time from depression. What was even worse was that it's intertwined with a heavy case of anxiety. Both of these working together are literally tearing me apart. One moment I care about everything, and the next minute I don't care about anything. I am wishing beyond belief to have this terrifying experience out of my head right now! Why is it that I'm constantly being pulled side to side from two extremities of frazzled emotion? Each day that passes is so fucking exhausting. My thoughts are draining me dry, tiring me every moment. My bed is now my closest friend at this point, and man, can I sleep. I've heard of people getting eating disorders and becoming insomniacs out of nowhere. But I am becoming one of those lost causes that could sleep through a category 5 hurricane. It's simply because I would rather be unconscious than awake." —January 6, 2015

What I'd like to share with you throughout this chapter is what we all have learned through living what I refer to as Practical Resilience. When you understand that you are going to hit the "Oh, shit" moments, and things will go haywire in life, there's a way to move through these times, and you will have the ability to do that.

Practical Resilience = Adversity * Mindset * Gratitude

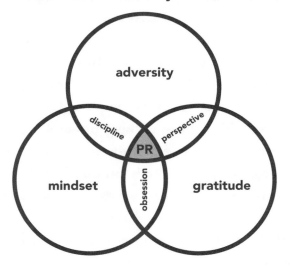

Let me explain how I discovered this formula. First, the three vital components are a multiplier of each, because when they're all in action, the result is exponential. But you can't just have one or two. You need all three for the best possible result. It's like having a pie without the crust. It's not going to taste right, and it will definitely taste like it's missing a key ingredient.

Simply, you can use the Practical Resilience toolkit in any facet of life that you want to make mentally unbreakable. Like a skill, it will take a great deal of practice, but when you continue with the concept until it becomes a habit, it won't feel like work after a couple months of daily repetition. Then, whenever you come across adversity, you will have the emotional intelligence to handle it.

Let's go into further detail and show you how the Practical Resilience formula works and the reasoning that's behind it.

ADVERSITY: PILLAR 1

To paint a picture, I'm going to mention a person who's had a tough life. It'll make you wonder how he came out alive. For those who haven't read the book or watched the movie, *Unbroken*, the story is about Louis Zamperini, a warrior who came across every possible torturous pitfall there could be. Louis was an American Olympian and even competed in the 1936 Berlin Games. But his sporting career didn't last as long as expected because several countries were undergoing political warfare, resulting in WW2. In those days, if you were a male over eighteen and relatively healthy, there was a possible chance you'd get drafted into the war to serve your country, which is exactly what happened. His role as a bomber plane shooter is definitely not for the thin skinned. He lived in a constant adrenaline-pumping state because he literally had to kill people while flying the plane.

Things were looking up when, all of a sudden, bang! Louis's plane got hit and crashed into the Atlantic Ocean where he and two teammates, Mac and Phil, were the only ones to survive the ocean landing. They floated on a raft no wider than two feet by six feet. In an emergency raft there is limited food and supplies, but Mac panicked during the first night and secretly ate all the food. Louis and Phil were frustrated beyond belief, because who knew how long they'd be floating while waiting to be rescued. In a situation like this, it's probably best not to piss everyone off, or you could get fed to the sharks.

Being resourceless is one thing, but being shot at from enemy planes, dealing with large ocean waves, and fighting off sharks in the process is another. At one particular moment, bullets from enemy planes pierced their raft, but thankfully, the bullets didn't penetrate all the way through.

However, their raft's surface was reduced by half. Three guys became two when Mac passed away from malnutrition and severe dehydration. It had been a challenge to remain alive during their thirty-three days on the raft. Louis bent over the side of the raft and gently slid Mac into the water. Mac sank quickly. The sharks let him be.

Phil and Louis could see the bend of their thighbones under their skin, their knees bulging in the centers of birdlike legs, their bellies hollow, their ribs stark. Each man had grown a weedy beard. Their skin glowed yellow from the leached raft dye, and their bodies were patterned with salt sores. They held their sun-scorched eyes to the horizon, searching for land, but there was none. Their hunger dimmed, an ominous sign. They had reached the last stage of starvation. How these brave men lasted another two weeks before they floated onto land was a miracle I'll never understand. They had spent forty-seven days with no food and water. To make matters worse, the raft floated into enemy Japanese territory. Surely, Louis thought the Japanese would kill them because they were so close. Instead, Louis was tortured by a Japanese general known as "The Bird" for another three years until the war ended. Louis endured an ultramarathon of anxiety, and he was crippled by horrific memories for years to come. He was beaten, whipped, burned, almost until he died. But somehow, he managed to live through the experience. To me, what he went through was unfathomable.

When Louis returned to America, all the trauma eventually caught up with him. He subsequently became addicted to alcohol and spent many years in hate-filled remorse, wondering what he did to deserve this. He sought help and eventually learned to let go of the past, but the hardest struggle was trying to remove the mental burden he suffered from, along with feeling like he had gone through hell and back. After three-plus years of sheer torture by the Japanese, he was reluctant to forgive the sadistic people who caused him so much grief. However, a "What if?" feeling arose in his gut and he wondered if going back there would remove all the pain. Months later, Louis returned to Japan to forgive "The Bird." Over time, from what was initially a psychological nightmare in loss of friends and well-being, Louis was able to live to ninety-seven years old. He came out a stronger man and now he has this amazing story to prove what doesn't kill you makes you stronger. You have to realize that for him to remain alive after all he went through was resilience at its finest.

From hearing Louis Zamperini's story, I'm going to explain the importance of adversity and why it's a good thing.

First of all, adversity is inevitable. Whether you're a high school student undergoing final exams, or you're a teacher, or a sixty-year-old CEO of a massive and thriving business, you'll go through stress no matter what. It's like saying pain is unavoidable. In this year alone, all of us have experienced either a heartbreak, a bruise, or a sense of sadness. Some individuals experience these feelings more than others, but it's 100 percent normal to suffer emotional pain.

Looking back at my struggles in 2014, the actual situations don't seem as bad now, but I believe my ability to recover was a result of the way I handled everything along with getting my negative thinking under control. I can't believe I put myself through such misery before I figured things out.

WHY DO WE REMEMBER THE NEGATIVE THINGS?

As mentioned in the previous chapter, humans are built for survival, and if we feel threatened, it could result in us retaliating without even realizing it. As a natural response, we try to protect ourselves because we still carry around logic from thousands of years ago. I know that if I endure a nasty comment or encounter an angry person, the way they act is not entirely their fault. They may be undergoing their own troubled past and are completely immobilized to retaliate because they're so close to the edge of losing it. Actually, they are a risk to others. What I'm about to say may surprise you or it may even scare you a little.

Any adversity is actually a blessing in disguise, believe it or not.

Why is that? How is something so negative going to become something great? Because you are all warriors, and grit is the proponent for growth. Every person you look up to in the world has gone through some sort of pain and that person has learned that you must be persistent, because everything happens for a reason. At the end of the day, it's going to be okay! At the moment you have the worst feeling and situation to endure, know that within a short time you will have overcome that pitfall! Then it becomes knowledge so when something similar happens again, you'll know exactly what to do. The experience can also let you help a friend who might be going through a tough time, similar to yours. Your help will be invaluable because you can relate to what your friend is feeling.

You may look at these moments as failures, but they're not failures. They're simply experiments that didn't go as planned. Overcoming every obstacle is the greatest strength you can obtain. Your neural pathways will be so accustomed to your response and attitude toward the situation that stress will become your best friend. It won't feel like a big deal, knowing your resilience is settling in like concrete. You're starting to become unbreakable. That is why greatness means rising above the turmoil, no matter how bad you have it.

From Michael Jordan growing into the GOAT of basketball, with an endless number of accolades even after his father was murdered, to the unfortunate experience that happened to a dear friend of mine who endured a leg amputation, just shows that we are much stronger and more resilient than we think we are.

KIRSTIE ENNIS IS A BRAVE EX-MARINE WHO WAS BLOWN UP FROM A HELICOPTER CRASH

Kirstie Ennis is an ex-Marine who lived to tell about her experience of being blown up in a helicopter crash. When we first met, Kirstie was in a limb salvage state, which meant she knew she'd be losing her leg. It was just a matter of time as to when it would happen. After ten reconstructive surgeries of her foot, she had avascular necrosis of the bones (a disrupted blood flow that makes the bones collapse and deteriorate) that in turn created nerve damage and severe pain. When Kirstie first returned home from Afghanistan with the injuries, doctors wanted to amputate her leg, but she refused and opted to attempt to save it. Knowing she would lose it soon, she did the 1,600 km trek to the UK as a sendoff for her leg, though she was heavily medicated to reduce the pain. Ten days after the walk, her leg was amputated below the knee. Then later, she got an infection in the hospital that required the surgeons to amputate above the knee.

Going from below the knee to above the knee in amputation is another kettle of fish. She went from a fixed prosthetic leg to a new leg with a mechanical knee. Eight months after the amputation, she signed up for the Augusta half-ironman triathlon and completed two marathons. But her heroism doesn't end there. Kirstie was a stunt double in two movies, *Patriots Day* with Mark Wahlberg on the Boston Marathon Bombings and the recent *Transformers* movie.

Another amputee friend of mine is Garry Rogers. He lost both arms during an electrical incident four years ago. Let's think about that: you've just lost your arms and practically every ability to do anything. I first met Garry back in 2016 while racing in running events, and I knew I wanted to know his story. He was a bit shy at first, but he's full of heart and such a nice guy—in addition to his funny sense of humor. As of June 2017, Garry and I completed a 100 km ultramarathon together. Long-distance running is more mental than physical. One moment you're steady, and the next moment you reach a mental challenge that holds you back. Somehow you just push through and come out with a finish. That's life, an ultramarathon! Even though Garry was struggling pretty badly in the last 10 km, he knew he would cross that finish line because he'd gone through worse times and had tackled his fears.

Both Kirstie and Garry have been through more trauma than anyone I've known personally. However, they both always have a smile on their faces, rarely complain, and they cherish every day like it's their last. You will rarely hear either of them ask, "Is it Friday yet?"

What's the best possible result you can obtain once you realize that adversity is a blessing in disguise? It's your mindset.

MINDSET: PILLAR 2

There is a study known as the "Marshmallow Test" that was created by Walter Mischel, who is a renowned psychologist. He conducted an experiment to learn how a child can resist immediate gratification. He and his team found a creative new way to observe this process in four-year-old children. Mischel and his team would bring the children into a room, one at a time, and they would show the child a marshmallow. Next, the child was offered a deal before they were left alone in the room. The children could eat the marshmallow whenever they wanted to, but if they held off until the experimenter returned, they would get a second marshmallow to eat along with it.

Some children gobbled the marshmallow right away; others tried resisting but couldn't hold out; yet others managed to wait the entire fifteen minutes for the bigger reward. By observing the children, something interested happened. Mischel noticed that the children who had failed to wait for the extra marshmallow seemed to get in more trouble than the others, both in and out of school. To see if there was a pattern to back up his theory, Mischel and his colleagues tracked down hundreds of veterans of the experiments. They found that the ones who had shown the most willpower at age four grew up to become more popular with their peers and their teachers. They earned higher salaries. They had a lower body-mass index, which suggested that they were less prone to gain weight as middle age encroached. In addition, they were less likely to have problems with drug abuse.

The importance of this anecdote is that it demonstrates how willpower and self-control are the foundation of having a killer-driven mindset. Having a six-pack body is great, but having a six-pack mind is even more incredible.

If you noticed, in the Marshmallow Test, strong willpower equates to strong discipline. People with good self-control seem exceptionally good at forming and maintaining secure, satisfying attachments to other people. It means you would be better at empathizing with others and considering things from other people's perspectives than someone who didn't have good self-control. Someone who has good mental and emotional stability is less prone to anxiety, depression, paranoia, psychoticism, obsessive compulsive behavior, eating disorders, drinking problems, and other afflictions.

Discipline makes you angry less often, and if you get angry, you have a less likely chance of getting verbally or physically aggressive. But to obtain strong discipline, you need a "reps and sets" mentality. This is a core aspect of growing in discipline that I've learned through one of my childhood idols, Arnold Schwarzenegger. Arnie is known for a great number of things, as I mentioned earlier.

But to get where he is, he had to develop consistent repetitions in specific activities so he could really hone in on those skills. Take body building; he'd work out six hours a day in his prime, because he knew to win Mr. Olympia he had to work harder than everyone else. The same thing applies to acting; he needed to take countless English-speaking classes to have a better chance at getting an acting role. Discipline is simple, but it isn't easy. With a strong mindset, you have to make sure you're not complaining whatsoever.

The grit you'll endure is part of the process. Each one of you must be able to handle the stress so, when you repeatedly work on something, you'll want to make sure there's no whining. Otherwise, you'll just attract more complainers into your life.

There will be days when you're not in the mood to work, whether it's a gym workout, eating healthier, or working on your dream. Your motivation might be at an all-time low, but this is when discipline and willpower will have to play their part. The point of discipline is to create positive habits so your reactions will come naturally and won't feel like work.

What's actually happening in the brain is it's creating automatic neural pathways. Picture a field of high grass, and once you take on a specific task, a row of grass is mown over and over to the point when a habit is created. When you brush your teeth each day, you're naturally drawn at a certain time to do it, because you've done it so many times in the past. So, apply the same principles with everything else you do in your life. It's also why we remember song lyrics so easily. You've sung that song or looked up the lyrics and read them over and over again. The result is that you can belt that song out because you've already memorized the words.

Discipline is one aspect of a strong killer-driven mind-set, but you can't be slow about putting it into action. Life is a game of speed chess; you have to be nimble while simultaneously making decisions. This is a trait I'm constantly working on or else I would overthink everything. Overthinking will drain you mentally and emotionally to a point where you become lazy and miserable. You can't let that happen, otherwise all the time you've invested will crumble and turn your good habits back into bad habits.

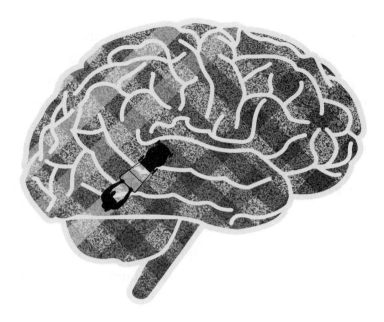

WHAT'S THE WORST THAT CAN HAPPEN?

If you come across a tough decision, simulate it with, "What's the worst thing that can happen?" Then, jump straight into it because you're battling fear head on. When you do this enough, then it becomes a habit. Once the habit is in place, you'll grow *thicker skin* to handle tough situations. And remember, if it didn't work out as expected, it's not failing. It's just an experiment that didn't go according to your plan.

When you create a new habit, you become an expert in that field. You've got this amazing momentum behind you and this strong sense of obsession. In addition, you'll feel kind of bulletproof. Literally, you'll feel invincible. This happened to me in May 2017, when I was in the Himalayas in Nepal. I got to climb a mountain in the Everest region that was just below Camp #2, which was without any supplementary oxygen. When we came upon several ladder-crossings over open crevasses, I knew I could easily make it to the other side. (A crevasse is an open crack that's caused by avalanches, and it's one of the main killers for climbers.)

Essentially, I was fearless. I had managed to train my mind those past couple of years through learning and conquering endurance tests. By putting myself in tough situations, on purpose, it made me mentally stronger. A tough task will result in one of these two responses: fear or trust. You can't have both. When I came to this moment where things could go very haywire along a crevasse ladder-crossing, resulting in death, fear was now my best friend. The neural pathway in my brain had built a strong habit of tackling immense challenges, and that task was just another event I knew I could conquer.

In a world of almost eight billion people, you have to stick out from the rest. So, why not be one of the mentally strong ones? You have an opportunity to be so good they can't ignore you.

With my proof-positive experiences with adversity, it has

helped me grow into a stronger person, but it wouldn't have happened without a killer-driven mindset. Even when things were so tough a few years ago, I'm unbelievably grateful for everything that's happened.

GRATITUDE: PILLAR 3

For those who don't know, I'm one-half of an endurance duo known as The Wounded Pelicans. We tackle absurd endurance events for various charitable causes. In 2016, with one of my best friends, Antony (Ant) Sedman, we completed forty events for cancer research. To put that into perspective, that's more than one every two weeks! We also entered events such as 100 km (63 mi.) ultra-marathons and running twenty-four hours on a treadmill.

At first, this project was intended to get us physically fit and raise funds for a cause that meant the world to us. We knew we would have media exposure that could easily benefit the cause with its awareness and donations. We originally had thirteen events planned, but things spiraled into forty. It was an adventurous year, to say the least.

It wasn't until we were eight months into the project that I had an a-ha moment I'll always remember like it was yesterday. Knowing I was truly making an impact felt so damn good, and I'm so grateful for that opportunity. Strangers we've never met before and friends with cancer would be thanking us for a long time, because we gave them a feeling of hope by assuring them we would be there for them. We knew nothing about cancer research, but by running thousands of kilometers for their cause, it would be our way of helping. People with cancer are incredibly strong because they battle a very rigorous war; running all those kilometers wasn't as tough as they had it.

PRACTICING DAILY GRATITUDE

Showing gratitude every single day is the fastest way to change your definition of reality. I've come to realize that when there are eight billion people in the world, we have a chance to learn how to put the practice of gratitude into perspective to create empathy for others. Don't try blaming others. Instead, think about how it feels to live in their circumstances rather than feeling sorry for yourself or getting angry at someone. You could think to yourself, "I'm having a tough time right now, but it's not all that bad compared to someone else's problems."

A perfect example is my blind friend, Damo, who lost sight in both eyes at a young age. When I initially heard about Damo in the running community, I was fortunate to meet him and hear his story firsthand. He lost his sight in both eyes due to separate accidents. He was so depressed, he became eighty-eight pounds overweight. Deciding to do something about it, Damo took up shotput to focus his energy in other things. Within a couple months, he held the Australian record for shotput. What an achievement! But he wasn't done yet. Still relatively overweight, his next goal needed something to help him slim down. That's when the treadmill became his best friend. He's clocked over 53,000 kms on it! He started his exercise routine by walking 27 km per day. Then, once he had a little more trust, he'd run 27 km per day.

For a while, I was Damo's guide runner once a week. I was responsible for getting him out of the house and we'd run on terrain that wasn't a conveyor belt. What an experience that was! He started noticing things like his hand placement, and he improved when we were both running in sync. If anyone gets the chance to guide a blind runner, it's a surreal feeling and an awesome experience. Just be sure that your awareness levels are on point or you might run him into a parked car, or at the very least, he might get knocked over by running into a car's side mirror. Also, watch out for pot holes in the street. Your runner won't be able to alter his path in time to avoid a fall.

My most memorable time with Damo was in March 2017, when I had to run in an event for twenty-four hours around a 400 m track. The event was for a family who had lost their dad to a heart attack, so whatever funds we could raise would be theirs to keep, which would help them get back on track.

While telling Damo about this event, I insisted he come down and run a few laps with a guide runner who wasn't me, since I had to focus on running for twenty-four hours. It turned out that his guide runner didn't show up, so I quickly came to the decision that I would be Damo's guide runner during my own twenty-four-hour race. A few laps turned into more than 130 laps. We legitimately clocked 50 km together, and I managed to put down 162.5 km by the time the twenty-four-hour challenge was over!

But running with a blind person like Damo, someone who's had it tough, always keeps me grounded because I feel rich in health. This is someone who literally can't see, so any everyday task becomes a mission. The thing is, Damo is always smiling, and he's the life of the party. He understands that you can't reverse time, so he focuses on the present. If I'm ever having a bad day, I use the perspective of picturing myself in Damo's shoes. I often wonder what it would be like waking up each morning, and even jumping in the shower or eating breakfast, without being able to see. Being blind would be such a difficult challenge. With that mental perspective, I instantly realize my day isn't that bad.

When we realize something has been taken away from us that we took for granted, it makes us much more grateful for what we have in this moment. In my opinion, the most grateful people in the world are the poorest. I've been lucky to have traveled to thirty countries, and many were developing countries and resourceless. I'll never forget when I explored the Favelas—the slums of Brazil. I met a gentleman dressed in ragged clothing who was missing an arm and a leg on the same side of his body. He invited me into his home and offered me food. I wondered how this guy could be so generous when he hardly had anything? I reasoned it was because he knew what it's like to have nothing and was happy to have the fundamentals in life—food, shelter, water, and his family. As a productive minimalist, he had everything he needed.

I'm reminded of an endurance event I recently did where I had to carry a brick for thirty-two hours. The event was a WWI commemoration for the one-hundred-year anniversary, with the name of a fallen soldier emblazoned on the brick. This 100 km trek was a team project where we'd walk through a steep forest, while it was raining, for twenty-one hours. By 3:00 a.m., I felt wrecked and so tired, but that's when I realized I didn't have it as bad as the WWI soldiers who had to endure gunfire, PTSD, and missing limbs. Their battles were tougher than a tiresome thirty-two-hour trek. It always comes back to your "why" during these tough times, and I guess I'm just grateful to have a bed to sleep on each night.

What I've learned is if you give back somehow—whether through a charity, a voluntary deed for a friend, or just being selflessly kind—favor will be given to you. Reciprocity takes place and you receive one hundred times more opportunities for kindness to come to you than you could ever imagine. That's why I believe there's an imbalance in the world right now. We have plenty of smart people, but we need a massive influx of kind people to override all the negative things happening in today's society.

Altruism, selflessness, or whatever you want to call it, is an art. You can't do something kind and expect a massive breakthrough to happen instantly. It has to come as an act from your heart, and it certainly has to be genuine; but, if you keep working on it as a primary trait, then it grows on you. It helps build your character, and you never know whose life you'll save. Hell, it might even be your own.

And that's what happened with me. Endurance and gratitude stopped me from taking my own life because of all the heavy depression and anxiety I was battling.

The last few years have been quite an experience. When I first decided to raise money through the endurance group I belong to, we chose $20,000 as part of the endurance-for-cancer project as the target goal. We thought thirteen events in one year wouldn't be enough, so it made sense for us to do twenty events—twenty in twenty. That escalated quickly because we pushed it to forty by the end of the year! Competing in more than one endurance event every two weeks is one thing, but raising $20,000 is something else. "How hard could it be to raise $20,000?" was said so nonchalantly when we decided to take this project on. How hard could it be? Well, if it was the easiest of tasks, then everyone would be doing it.

I hope this inspires you to help those who really need it. If you've ever wanted to raise money for a cause that means a lot to you, then do it. You'll be surprised how far you can really go. It feels really good when you reach your target!

In 2015, Antony and I had completed eight running events, and this sparked the great idea of continuing to run one event a month in 2016—but this time, for a cause. We decided to run for the cause of cancer research because we had both lost family to cancer. We didn't think anything of it at the time, but raising $20K for cancer research was not easy!

When you put your body through forty endurance events, it is physically and mentally draining. **YOU SACRIFICE ALMOST EVERYTHING** because it's one hell of a commitment. Almost every weekend, we were awake at some sort of "stupid o'clock" for training or events. But hey, if it was easy, then everyone would be doing it. As tough as my year had been, it was also a fun year! Our training schedule changed every week to adapt to the upcoming events of that weekend.

Long-distance running was the prominent focus, and it took multiple 100 km ultramarathons, obstacle course races, and even a twenty-four-hour treadmill challenge! For those who didn't know us prior to our endurance alias, The Wounded Pelicans, we were known as the typical party kids who spent the majority of our weekends drinking and writing ourselves off of any other agenda. I was never a runner to begin with, which is ironic because endurance is what I'm known for these days.

MORE APPRECIATION FOR GRATITUDE

If there was one value in life I wish they taught kids in school, it would be the act of gratitude. Doing things for others has an exponential return on investment. Now, ROI doesn't necessarily have to be business related, but it can definitely be applied to health, well-being, relationships, and even spirituality.

What I'm saying is, "There's a magic in giving and being grateful."

Since taking up ultrarunning sports and various extreme endurance events, it's been a wild ride, in the best way possible. At first, I began running to improve my health. But actually, running became my escapism. Struggling with depression and anxiety at the time had taken a bite out of my mind. I knew I needed to get healthy. That's when I had the epiphany of training for a marathon. It was a large enough goal to keep my mind off things, yet, I didn't think it was possible to tackle a feat like that, especially since I had never been a runner to begin with!

After completing my first marathon in 2015, I became obsessed with running to improve my health and my state of mind. Even to this day, I'm still curious about the topic and it's created a newfound love inside me. It's become my passion.

I was fortunate to get my dear friend, Ant, to join me for these running events. We decided that for 2016, we'd run one event a month, but for a charity. Simply the thought of any decent exposure would be beneficial, and we knew it would help people along the way. Looking back, every one of our absurd ideas was either cultivated from a training run or over a beer.

As I mentioned earlier, we dedicated the entire year of 2016 to cancer research. Cancer is something that's affected both our families and it's still a massive issue today. We have no idea about how to cure cancer, but our way of helping is by putting our bodies through physical endurance challenges to raise money for those who truly need it.

There are those patients who are suffering and have it

much tougher than we do. That's the perspective that made running for a long period of time seem like a much easier task. During the days when you're feeling down, you have to remember your "why." When you can explain out loud your reason for taking up a challenge or an ambition from the start, then you have a goal to conquer. We didn't want to let the team down. So, this intertwined with our persistence to continue on when it was sometimes a struggle.

THE PURPOSE OF THE WOUNDED PELICANS AS DEFINED BY TWO NORMAL KIDS WHO WANTED TO MAKE A DIFFERENCE.

If you're wondering how we came up with the name The Wounded Pelicans, it was a name we came up with while in school, and we decided to roll with it because it's goofy like us. However, as the years have come and gone and we've both experienced crazy events, we realized that we were emulating a pod of pelicans, in the sense that it can "hold more in its beak" than appeared possible. This thinking translates into how we can endure more than a normal person running back-to-back events. During this past year, there were times when we were injured—which is where the "wounded" part comes into play—and times I was mentally messed up, which made me doubly wounded.

As you keep reading, you'll see how our name is now a

philosophy, since we continue to push the limits, helping others—similar to how a pod of pelicans can hold more in their beaks. Everything from back-to-back full marathons, to 160 km ultramarathons, to the infamous Kokoda Trail, to even a twenty-four-hour treadmill challenge was part of our endurance agenda.

We gained amazing traction and momentum, and we decided that it would be silly to throw in the towel in 2017. This brought up the question, "How do you top forty events?" Well, this is where it became important for us to focus on quality, not quantity.

Completing forty endurance events in one year was incredibly exhausting. We sacrificed almost every weekend, woke up at stupid o'clock for training, worked full-time jobs, got injured now and then, and hustled in our spare time for the backend side of things regarding the blog and social media. But it was totally worth it!

We made so many awesome friendships and our network is constantly growing—plus the bolder the task, the better the result and feeling.

Speaking of bold, that brings us to the 2017 endurance project. Remember how I said the focus would be on quality and not quantity? That meant taking on ten extreme endurance events, one a month from March to Decem-

THE BIG 10

THE WOUNDED PELICANS
2017 ENDURANCE PROJECT

10 'NOT-SO-TAME' EVENTS
ZERO LIMITS
ALL FOR YOUTH
OUT TO MAKE A DIFFERENCE

THE BIG 10
EVENT 1
24HR RUN

NO LIMITS ENDURANCE

WHERE? RUNAWAY BAY SPORTS SUPER CENTRE
1 SPORTS DR. RUNAWAY BAY QLD 4216
WHY (CAUSE)? FOR THE LOSS OF CRAIG PERCIVAL
NO LIMITS ENDURANCE ATHLETE
WHAT'S HAPPENING? LOTS OF RUNNING... SEE LINK
BELOW FOR MORE DETAILS

MAR 11-12 | 7AM-7AM

HTTP://WWW.THEWOUNDEDPELICANS.COM/24-HOUR-RUN-EVENT-1/

EVENT 2 | THE BIG 10
APRIL 21-23, 2017 | BOND UNI

48 HOUR ALTITUDE LOCKUP

Eat / Sleep / Train in a High Altitude Chamber
- University Research Study -
Raising funds for Youth Mental Health

BOND UNIVERSITY · headspace

THE WOUNDED PELICANS ? CURE?

MT EVEREST ULTRAMARA
EVENT 3 | THE BIG 10

WORLD'S HIGHEST ULTRA | 80KM | MAY 20, 2017
TO RAISE AWARENESS/ FUNDS TOWARD A CURE

MOJO · RESCUESWAG · Scrubba · BOND UNI

EVENT 4 | THE BIG 10 | THE WOUNDED PELICANS

100KM BLIND-AMPUTEE ULTRAMARA

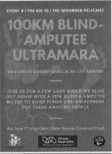

WE STAND IN SUPPORT OF ALL BLIND AND AMPUTEE

JOIN US FOR A FEW LAPS WHILE WE SLOG
OUT 100KM WITH A FEW BLIND & AMPUTEE
MATES TO RAISE FUNDS AND AWARENESS
FOR THESE AMAZING PEOPLE

8st June 17 | from 6am | Lake Runp Coomban Track

Vision Australia

"YOU HAVE THE POWER TO CHANGE STUFF"

100KM THANKYOU WATER WALK
EVENT 5 | THE BIG 10

TO RAISE ONE COPY OF
'CHAPTER ONE' BY DAN FLYNN

July 15-16 | Geelong to Collingwood
carrying 25kg of water on
shoulders for 100km | 24 hours
Representing the youth around
the world who have to travel to
collect water for their families.

RUN DOWN UNDER · thankyou.

THE BIG 10
EVENT 6
12HR SWIM

WHERE? BOND UNI INSTITUTE OF HEALTH & SPORT
2 PROMETHEAN WAY, ROBINA QLD 4226
WHY (CAUSE)? FOR OUR FUTURE LIFESAVERS
NIPPER'S BEACH / OFF-LIFE NIPPERS
WHAT'S HAPPENING? LOTS OF SWIMMING... SEE LINK
BELOW FOR MORE DETAILS

AUG 19 | 4AM-4PM

https://www.thewoundedpelicans.com/event-6-12hr-swim/

BOND UNIVERSITY

The Wounded Pelicans presents...

THE BIG 10
EVENT 7
80KM SUP
(STAND UP PADDLEBOARD)

SAT SEPT 23 2017 | 5AM TILL WE FINISH.
KURRA BEACH, GOLD COAST
OPEN TO ANYONE TO JOIN US :)

DEDICATED TO ALL THE YOUTH BATTLING
IT TOUGH WITH ANY SORT OF ADVERSITY
https://www.thewoundedpelicans.com/event-7-80m-stand-paddle/

MOJO · Buzvil · SURF FX

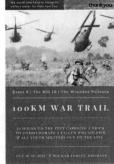

Event 8 | The BIG 10 | The Wounded Pelicans

100KM WAR TRAIL

32 HOURS ON THE FEET CARRYING A BRICK
TO COMMEMORATE A FALLEN WW1 SOLDIER
& ALL YOUTH MILITARY OUT ON THE LINE

OCT 16-17, 2017 | D'AGUILAR FOREST, BRISBANE

EVENT 9 OF THE BIG 10

465

To raise awareness for wheelchair bound youth!

November 1 - 30
Everyday we add on an extra km
465km completed by Nov 30
Join, run, and be apart of the movement!

RUN DOWN UNDER

Check www.thewoundedpelicans.com/465 for more details.

PELICA

EVENT 10 OF THE BIG 10

50KM SANTA RUN

Running the GC50 (K20) in Santa suits!

Dedicated to the kids who don't get to
experience Xmas this year

SUN 10 DEC | KURRAWA | 2017 FINALE

ber, which left the first two months of the year open for relaxing our bodies after an intense 2016.

This project was known as THE BIG 10.

Not only do each of the events contain some sort of extreme physical and emotional endurance, but each month correlates with a different cause for struggling youths.

Maybe you're wondering why we are so committed to helping youths? It's simply because they'll be the future creators and innovators of the world we live in. Not only that, but we want to teach them how to stay healthy. We want them to push their limits, and we want them to understand how important gratitude is, especially when they're learning to pay things forward. To be known as a young athlete in the community automatically shows how youthful I am myself. So, by being a spokesperson and a young thought leader on resilience and mental health, I'm hopeful that by what I'm doing to help our youth, it's inspiring to them. I want them to have big dreams.

One of the ten events involved the most danger and risk— Event 3, which entailed a massive journey over to Mt. Everest, tackling a 60 km ultramarathon from Everest Base Camp, the world's highest ultramarathon.

Our goal was to raise funds for a cure for Cystic Fibrosis

(CF). Why? It is an intense journey, since I'll have less than 50 percent oxygen available during the run. This correlates to what it's like to be a Cystic Fibrosis patient on a day-to-day basis.

For those unaware, Cystic Fibrosis is the most common, life-shortening, genetic condition that affects young Australians today. A baby is born with Cystic Fibrosis every four days! The condition affects the lungs, digestive system, and sweat glands, requiring relentless, expensive daily physiotherapy and medical regimes.

It's important to note that there is currently NO cure, and the average life expectancy for those born with CF is thirty-eight years. Because there is no cure, it is quite an issue, and it's not fair for the parents and the youth of today who have CF.

Going back to the topic of gratitude, since I've started helping people, it's become another newfound love, passion #2. It amazes me every day how some sort of adversity can become a blessing in disguise. The fact that a combination of these two passions (endurance and helping others) is what I live and breathe every day. It's my purpose in life.

EVERYONE NEEDS SOME GRATITUDE IN THEIR LIFE

You can't package gratitude and it's definitely invaluable if you can offer it to those who truly need it. Everyone can apply gratitude in their life, but they don't need to run thousands of kilometers to make their point. If you feel like pushing the limits in ways unimaginable, like I did, then maybe running thousands of kilometers for others will strengthen your mental game. Whenever and wherever you can show kindness and help others, you are helping them understand the true meaning of gratitude and being grateful.

I believe we need more kindness and giving in the world today. The beauty of this is that you can take action immediately. Here are a few things you can do today:

1. Call a friend or family member and tell them how much their friendship means to you.
2. Write a list of three things every morning that explains what you're grateful for. This action step will keep you in a positive mood; and remember, positivity is key and it rubs off on people.
3. Get behind a friend's charity project or new business venture, because they're trying to do good for this world and make an impact.
4. Capture all gratifying moments into a "gratitude journal." This is important, so you can reflect on these thoughts when you're going through future adversity. It will remind you of the good times.
5. Commit to running in a local charity race or marathon if you're up for the challenge. Then, dedicate the funds and create an awareness to a cause bigger than yourself.
6. Focus on the things you have and not on the things you think are missing in your life. This will instantly make you grateful, and it will shift your thinking from scarcity mode to an abundance mindset.
7. Introduce yourself to new acquaintances with, "How can I help you?" instead of "Hey, would you know who's hiring?" The first response offers value and shows how proactive you are for wanting to help that person. Maybe he or she will reciprocate when you least expect it.
8. Be empathetic. Listen to those who are reaching out for

help. Maybe you've gone through a situation similar to theirs and you can understand why they're not in the best place right now. Your conversation may be the catalyst that saves them from doing anything stupid.

9. Watch your language and what you say to others because it can trigger an angry response, which defeats your purpose of showing gratitude to others.

10. Understand that the past is the past and you can't reverse time. It's okay to acknowledge the lessons you can learn to prevent that situation from happening again. This isn't the easiest of tasks, but after enough repetition, you will feel grateful for how far you've come.

Life's too short to be hating anyone, so why not spread more love and kindness? When you start treating everyone the same, no one will feel worthless. Why should you treat a high-profile athlete differently than an everyday civilian? They're both human beings. They both deserve to have gratitude shown to them.

GRATITUDE MAKES US HAPPY

There's a difference between altruism and people-pleasing, because if we're truly being authentic, pure altruism brings a sense of self-compassion, an inner lens to look through to see what we're grateful for. We start the gratitude process by giving and helping others, which extends out to the world. It differs from people-pleasing because it can have an opposite effect. For example, when a company takes on a project just to impress people and make it look like they truly care about a cause, but they don't, it's not the same as someone who genuinely shows gratitude. The company, in this example, expects something in return. Whereas a truly grateful individual or company does it to help and does not expect anything in return.

When building our gratitude practice, we're shifting our mental focus in our brain from things in jeopardy to what's going well. After enough practice, we start taking better care of ourselves and, by nature, we also take care of others. Plus, it feels good, and there's a stronger reconnection with ourselves intrinsically. The bottom line is that gratitude is the fastest way to change your definition of reality.

CASE STUDIES

Following are three examples of case studies that reflect the Practical Resilience formula that we use in real life.

NIGEL FARROW

Dr. Nigel Farrow entered into the medical profession when his daughter was diagnosed with Cystic Fibrosis ten years ago in 2006. His single focus was to be part of the team that was developing a cure for this disease. Nigel gave up his career, began seven years of study, and obtained a Bachelor of Medical Science degree at Flinders University, a Bachelor of Health Science with first-class honors at the University of Adelaide, and a PhD in medicine, also at the University of Adelaide.

Along the way, Nigel received a number of awards, including a Dean's award for PhD excellence, The Pride of Australia medal, and a letter of commendation for dedication, passion, and a commitment to the community through research from Martin Haese, Lord Mayor of Adelaide, South Australia, 2015.

Now a medical scientist and part of the Adelaide Cystic Fibrosis Airway Research Group, Nigel is helping to find a cure for Cystic Fibrosis airway disease. He wants this for his daughter and the seventy thousand other people who suffer from the disease globally. Nigel's research is focused on correcting the genetic cause of Cystic Fibrosis at a cellular level in the airways. To achieve this, a modified virus is used as a transport mechanism to introduce a healthy copy of the Cystic Fibrosis gene into the airway cells.

Not only is the gene inserted into the cell, but the virus was chosen because it has the ability to insert the gene into the genome of the recipient, which allows stable gene integration for the life of the cells. The next step is that the cells have a lifespan, so they are eventually lost and the procedure has to be repeated. To combat the loss of the cells, he is developing a way to target the adult stem cells that live in the airway and will replace the cells as they die off as a natural process.

By targeting the airway stem cells for inserting a healthy copy of the CF gene, it will then pass on the healthy CF gene to his daughter's cells. This has the potential of providing a means to prevent Cystic Fibrosis airway disease with a single treatment early in life that will last for the lifetime of the patient.

Nigel's work has been accepted and published in the greater scientific community through peer reviewed scientific journal publications. Nigel has also been invited to present his work at conferences in Australia, New Zealand, the United Kingdom, and the USA.

I'm happy that I've had the pleasure of knowing Nigel when I was at the Cystic Fibrosis research lab in Adelaide in April 2017. I was there just a month before heading to the Himalayas to run down Everest to raise funds for CF. Such a genuine soul, Nigel is one driven guy who wants to find a cure for Cystic Fibrosis so his daughter and many others can live without being in so much pain.

HURRICANE HARVEY

Natural disasters are the hardest to plan for because you honestly can't predict what Mother Nature might do, regardless of calculated predictions. On August 17, 2017, a harmful tropical Atlantic hurricane destroyed several towns in Texas and Louisiana. All power was lost, houses were flooded, and lives were taken. Everyone knew how real Hurricane Harvey was.

With what looked like a bomb had hit those regions, the love and outpouring of help from around the country and the world came or sent food, water, clothing, and offered shelter for individuals, families, pets, cattle, and horses. This was indeed an uncontrollable disaster and a stressful time for everyone.

The cities and residents affected by the hurricane were devastated. So many people were displaced and lost their homes and their precious belongings. But after the hurricane had left the area, people dropped everything to help each other out. No one disparaged race, age, gender, color, or sexuality. Everyone was willing to help each other during a highly stressful time. A furniture store used its beds for shelter; Anheuser-Busch, a brewery based out of Georgia, sent 155,000 cans of emergency water; civilians rescued many people with boats; even a doughnut shop kept its doors open so any struggling civilians could get food if they'd lost everything.

The ones who suffered the most from the hurricane will always remember those times, especially when the community did what they could to get everyone back on their feet. Yes, there was the realization that many had hit rock bottom, though there was also greatness and compassion cultivated throughout this trajectory of pain.

LIVIN ORGANISATION

Sam Webb and Casey Lyons are two Australian friends who have built a name for themselves on the Gold Coast and around Australia. It all started when one of their best friends, Dwayne Lally, was found dead in 2013, after committing suicide. When suicide claims someone you love, the desire to stop others from taking the same fatal step can be overpowering. It was for Casey Lyons when he walked into the Gold Coast Hospital morgue in September 2013. "They pulled the curtain back and there was Dwayne," says Lyons. Dwayne Lally, twenty-four, Lyons's best friend since their first day of primary school, had killed himself. "It hit me straightaway that I had to do something," says Lyons.

From there, LIVIN was founded in honor of Casey and Sam's great friend, Dwayne Lally, who, like many others, took his life after suffering in silence from a mental illness. LIVIN is all about living your life at the top and destroying the stigma that is attached to mental illness. Their purpose is dedicated to connecting, supporting, and encouraging one another to talk about their feelings, issues, and challenges, because, "It Ain't Weak to Speak." Out with the old and in with the new, LIVIN was created to shake things up and make it okay to speak up and seek help in the twenty-first century. There's no judgment, just sheer compassion and understanding. Through education programs and awareness initiatives, LIVIN will launch a generational change. Let's unite to help our brothers and sisters start LIVIN again. Join the movement.

The LIVIN story blossomed out of a tragic moment, but it created a foundation for those who are experiencing mental health struggles. They are encouraged to open up and become more vulnerable. That's what resonated with me to begin this book project with LIVIN. Even though Casey and Sam have lost a dear friend, they've become incredibly thankful for where they are now. Their message on mental health is truly making an impact and is helping others to open up. The impact LIVIN has made on mental health is the reason why I am dedicating 10 percent of ALL book sales to one of their programs. I've seen it work firsthand with not only my own life, but with some of my closest friends.

HOW THE PRACTICAL RESILIENCE FORMULA CAN HELP YOU

There are three situations that can take you from being in a rut to living your best life!

STUCK IN A JOB YOU HATE WHEN YOU KNOW YOU HAVE A PASSION THAT WILL LEAD TO YOUR PURPOSE?

Are you currently waking up every day wishing it was the weekend already? If so, this is a great indicator you're stuck in the wrong profession and in need of a career shift. You can make the excuse that you have this job because you need to pay your bills and you have a family to feed. We all do. Just remember, life is made for living and not just for paying the bills. You're probably dealing with anxiety because you have to work with a crazy boss and shitty coworkers. Or, maybe your self-confidence is lacking but you realize this is only going to be temporary, as long as YOU do something about it.

Your best bet is to create a side hustle around any area that you're curious about, like a hobby or developing a skill you've thought about for years. Just do it. Invest some of your spare time learning and experimenting. Yes, you do need to spend time with your family and kids, but rather than sitting in front of your TV or an electronic device, you can spend time in your side hustle curiosity project. Then, when you have some momentum in the works and small victories are happening on a frequent basis, AND you're making enough money, these might be signs to quit the job you hate. Have you considered turning your side hustle into a full-time gig? When you decide to launch your new career, you'll be so grateful and appreciative with how far you've come in a short amount of time that you won't care if it's the weekend or Tuesday. You will like waking up every morning knowing you're doing something you're passionate about.

In Chapter 10, you'll learn more about your job transition, but before you can make that important life change, you need to read the chapters leading up to it so you can understand the required groundwork.

DEALING WITH THE DEATH OF A CLOSE FRIEND OR FAMILY MEMBER

When someone close to you dies, it's a tough moment to live through, and we all wish the circumstance never existed. But no one lives forever, unfortunately. When this news reaches you, it breaks your heart and every melancholic emotion hits you harder than a bus rolling down a mountain at full speed. Everything about that person reminds you of the great times you had, and then you suddenly experience a severe sense of loss. You go through all sorts of feelings and you secretly wish you could've done something to prevent it from happening. But then something magical happens during this gloomy period; it brings everyone together.

I remember when my grandma died in September 2016. My parents were at an all-time low. The funeral took place in the Philippines in my grandma's hometown. My entire family was there for each other. Then, instantly, I had a sense of thankfulness that seemed to be shared by everyone around me. We were so grateful for each other. Even though it's painful when we lose someone close to us, it brings family and friends together and makes us appreciative of each other.

LIVING WITH THE REALITY THAT YOUR BUSINESS IS BEING CLOSED FOR GOOD

I've experienced this situation a couple times, but the first time it happened, I freaked out. I somehow managed to stay calm the second time, simply because I had learned to look at this failure like an experiment that didn't go as planned. Believe it or not, Bill Gates and Paul Allen launched a company, Traf-O-Data, a data reporting business they believed would take off that actually turned into a total bust due to a poor business model and very few customers.

Fast forward to 1975, two years later. Gates had dropped

out of Harvard Business School and planned to focus his energy on a new venture with Allen—Microsoft. What the dynamic duo learned from what didn't work with Traf-O-Data they applied to the creation of Microsoft, which arguably was the most successful and prolific technology company in its prime. I bet Gates and Allen probably look back at their Traf-O-Data days and feel glad they endured it, because Microsoft wouldn't be the same without learning from what they had done the first time.

As for me, my other business ventures didn't go as planned, but the current one I'm working on is much stronger and more stable. It's built on a foundation of what I learned from the failures of previous ventures. For sure, experience is the best teacher.

CHAPTER 4

SELF-AWARENESS AND SELF-ACCEPTANCE

"It's a warm evening on a spring day but there's been no sunshine seen from these eyes in months. Hunched over on a park bench; popping another antidepressant shifts the uncontrollable angst, a state of nothingness. Wondering if I'm alone in this moment and doing everything I can to control every nerve from breaking down, then all of a sudden, a puddle of tears streams down my face. The dry vandalized picnic table went from a light pine timber to a saturated mahogany. This wasn't a loud cry, full of expression. It was more of a hidden scream for help, with me wondering how I got to this point in my life." —Jan 14, 2015

TOFE: Lewis, if there was one piece of advice you could give your younger self, what would it be?

LEWIS HOWES: Acknowledge yourself for what you have created in your life and be nice to yourself. I spent so much of my growing up years angry, sad, frustrated, and beating myself up. I didn't realize how damaging that was until I started to unpack all that.

HOW MANY OF US HAVE SPENT COUNTLESS YEARS TRYING TO SILENCE THOSE THOUGHTS IN OUR HEAD?

For me, I wasted a lot of years on this concept. Through my curiosity, however, I discovered it's incredibly ineffective to spend your entire life trying to make those inner demons shut up. Instead, you can harness those sneaky bastards and get them to push you forward in life. Paradoxically speaking, the mind is one of the most intricate and complex systems we deal with every day. The survival aspect of our brain is constantly trying to help us, but our mind is our greatest driver for doing things, some of which we don't like. You can actually do anything; it's the limits we put on ourselves that hold us back.

HOW DO I GET THE WIN-WIN, SO I DON'T BECOME A LOSER?

If you don't understand how the body works, you'll never have good health. If you don't understand anything about money, you'll never be financially independent. If you don't understand your strengths, you'll struggle with propelling yourself forward. These seem like simple rules, however, *simple* is sometimes too much for the average person to understand because they want to complicate everything.

"To know a species, look at its fears. To know yourself, look at your fears. Fear in itself is not important, but fear stands there and points you in the direction of things that are important. Don't be afraid of your fears, they're

not there to scare you; they're there to let you know that something is worth it."

—C. JOYBELL C.

It really comes down to self-awareness. You must know what makes you tick, your strengths and weaknesses, and what drives you.

If you have no idea who you are, that's okay, you're not alone. The signs are actually in front of you without you even realizing it. Here are three simple personality tests that will show you what you need to know about yourself:

1. MYERS-BRIGGS. This test reveals how you perceive the world around you and defines how you make decisions.
2. FOUR TENDENCIES. This test determines how you typically react to expectations.
3. DISC. Take this test when you want to find your communication style.

Even though these tests are different, try all three! There

will be questions you might be uncomfortable answering though. The key is you need to be 100 percent brutally honest to get the best possible outcome. Note, there are no right or wrong results.

You'll come across synergies and figure out what you're naturally good at, so triple down on these bad boys! But it doesn't end there. You'll recognize what your weaknesses are too. You'll also learn about your strengths, depending on where you spend the most time.

There's no law of physics saying you can't distribute what you're not good at. I highly encourage involving your team members during this process. For every successful or great person that's lived, they'll tell you they couldn't do it all on their own.

How much more productive are we when we're taking on a task we're good at? Known as flow, Mihaly Csikszent-mihalyi, a social psychologist who discovered to concept, explains that it's the state we enter when time flies and you fall into a cadence of fluid motion. During *flow*, people typically experience deep enjoyment, creativity, and a total involvement with life.

But what about the things we don't want to do that we suck at?

If you've come to a point in your life where you want to focus on what you are naturally great at, then partner with someone who will bring the skills to the table that you heavily lack. By recognizing our strengths and weaknesses, we become acceptant of who we are, which allows us to focus on maximizing our full potential. Whether it's data entry, creating websites, building networks, or analyzing research reports, there's always something out there that another person can help you with.

I completely agree that we should recognize them according to the personality tests mentioned earlier, though there is an effective situation that works wonders. It's called collaboration. There are many other terms for collaborators: teammates, partners, freelancers, business developers, coworkers, third parties, etc. But when you allow yourself to collaborate with another human who has strengths and skills that you don't have, it's a win-win result.

We live in a collaborative world, and it's almost impossible to avoid meeting another person whom you're meant to connect with. My own experiences of teaming up with universities, Shark Tank-invested companies, and emerging brands have been such an eye-opener. The following lessons can serve as takeaways for your own situation:

- Everyone wants the same result and end goal—trust is strengthened when you help each other out, whenever possible.
- It's a winning combination when you're introduced and referred to an entirely new network.
- It makes it easier for credibility when you're associated with well-established brands.
- You'll get more opportunities for new work when people can see your previous work.

HOW DO WE COLLABORATE?

The way we partner up is by knowing what the other parties are trying to achieve and creating an outcome that can benefit everyone on all sides. To give you an understanding of how prevalent the concept is, the following list is an example of working collaborations you may recognize.

- GoPro and Red Bull
- McDonald's and Uber Eats
- Caltex Socceroos
- UFC, Reebok, and EA Sports
- BMW and Berlin Marathon

Maybe you're in a position where you are starting out or looking to diversify, but you have a tight budget. Or maybe you're just not well-recognized in your field yet, and that's okay too! Concerning my experiences with collaborating, I've learned it's a work-in-progress. You may not get GoPro on board straightaway, but with enough practice, you will eventually catch their attention. Following are three hypothetical situations that you may encounter that will help you collaborate and grow your brand or business. (Note: I have experienced all three of these.)

1. ASPIRING BLOGGER. After blogging for the last two years, I've noticed that page views will increase quite substantially if I interview someone renowned in the field, because there's a chance they'll reshare the post with their own social channels.

2. BUSINESS PLATEAU. To stand out in business you need great marketing, otherwise it will result in financial turmoil faster than getting the business registered. It can suck big time when your marketing efforts fail, especially when you don't have much of a budget as you're growing your business. That's why it's worth reaching out to larger brands and seeing how you can somehow work with them, because they'll help promote and introduce you to an entirely new network of connections. This could ultimately lead to future collaboration and new clients.

3. HOSTING AN EVENT. This one can be fun because

it's cost-effective if it's done right. You will need to get the right sponsors on board. Logistics and planning are the stressful part, but acquiring sponsors to come on board could easily benefit your efforts if their brand is shown throughout the event and shared on social media. They might not want to give you funding, but they might agree to supplying a venue, product, or some sort of sweat equity. Keep working on that relationship when your sponsorship arises, and it may turn into them giving you financial backing at a later time.

I know I can't work FOR people, especially those who have no vision, but I do work WITH people really well when our purposes align. It's okay to work for people, even if you're more knowledgeable than the CEO, but the point is to ensure that the overall path leads to greatness as opposed to working on something just for the sake of it. It is absolutely imperative that you understand your strengths and know where you stand to really create an environment where you don't care what day it is. Remember, you're on a mission to win!

Based on my results with the three personality tests mentioned earlier, I know the areas I need improvement in and where I need help. Because I am emotionally driven, I can work my arse off because there's not much motivation required. Where I am heavily lacking, however, is in structure. Superlatively, I can get something off the ground quite easily. I can maintain consistency, and I can create an endless plethora of options. However, if a system and procedures aren't in place, I'm short-sighted and suffer from Myopia.

Since I am now aware of this, I can put the right team of business coaches and strategy specialists together to prevent me from making any silly mistakes. Hey, it's okay to make mistakes, but they don't have to be yours! That's why we have mentors.

There's no law saying how many mentors you can have. If anything, the more, the merrier. There won't be any one person who will have all the answers. My business strategist isn't my strength or endurance coach and vice versa. It's as if these key people have their focus in one field and they are masters at what they do. This is a great benefit for me, because it's better to be really great at one thing than mediocre at a thousand things.

ACCEPTING WHO YOU ARE AS A PERSON

It's important that you embrace yourself for who you are as a person!

"Cows, after you've seen them for a while, are boring. They may be perfect cows, attractive cows, cows with great personalities, cows lit by beautiful light, but they're still boring. A Purple Cow, though. Now that would be interesting. (For a while.) The essence of the Purple Cow is that it must be remarkable. If you're remarkable, it's likely that some people won't like you. That's part of the definition of remarkable. Nobody gets unanimous praise— ever. The best the timid can hope for is to be unnoticed. Criticism comes to those who stand out."

—SETH GODIN

Believe it or not, my first name is Christopher, which will probably have you wondering, "Where on earth did you get 'Tofe'?"

Well, it's my nickname, my persona, and my true identity. Pronounced "Toaf" and it rhymes with loaf, it's what I've been called by almost everyone for the last ten years, and it's a nickname I've had since high school.

Long story short, it's been my nickname since grade eleven, and where Chris and Christopher were too prevalent, it was easier to have something simpler and different. I was later called "Topher," as in the last half of Christopher, which soon became "Tofa," and now it's just "Tofe." It's pretty unique, as I'm the only Tofe Evans in Facebookland and the interwebs.

We all have that friend who gets called by their nickname and it sounds weird to even say their real name. I'm that *friend*. Honestly, 95 percent of the people I know have never known me as Chris or Christopher. Christopher Evans is a common name, and you know Captain America? He's even got the same name.

Since I've had clarity regarding my vision and purpose in life these past couple years, I've been grateful to have seen my dream go from concept to reality. One dream was to be a keynote speaker, though it makes things difficult when a person hears that "Christopher Evans is delivering a keynote tonight," and the audience expects to see the human torch from Fantastic Four.

Since I exist as the only Tofe Evans in the world, this helps immensely with personal branding. Not to digress, but when I hear the name Christopher Evans, it sounds boring and seems to lack adventure. Tofe is much more than a nickname; it represents what I'm about and connects with what I do, including my values and purpose.

I've learned to embrace my own Purple Cow.

You've probably realized how conspicuous my progress has been as I've gone from rock bottom to where I am today. As I began my journey, I was hungry to win and make outstanding progress. I didn't focus on how I was progressing compared to others because my journey was different than theirs. I'm only in competition with myself, which equates to **ME** vs. **ME**. It's okay to reflect on the greats and emulate what they've done and the resilience they've acquired from great adversity, but I feel it's not worth comparing myself to them because each of us has a much different and unique story.

You might not be the strongest, fastest, or smartest person out there, but it's not any of those qualities that help you get the most out of life. It's the ones who can **adapt** the quickest and bounce back after every fall. You may have a weird personality and still watch Disney movies, but who cares? No one is judging you. If you're thinking you have it worse than most people, embrace it and move on.

KATRINA WEBB, AUSTRALIAN SPORTING LEGEND

Katrina is no stranger to a gold medal podium or a star-lit stage. She has received awards and medals most athletes only dream about. Despite this success, her journey hasn't always been easy. Born into a family of sporting stars, it was no surprise that young Katrina Webb possessed natural athleticism. By the age of eighteen, she had already secured a netball scholarship at The Australian Institute of Sport. What she didn't realize at that time was her sporting career was about to take an unexpected turn.

During training at the Institute of Sport, Katrina was informed she had a weakness in her right side, which turned out to be a case of Cerebral Palsy. Katrina's ability to pursue netball at a national level was now in jeopardy. Despite this, a twist of fate presented a previously unseen opportunity. Katrina was now eligible for the Paralympic games. Her weakness had become her greatest strength.

Over the years, Katrina had tried to conceal her disability, so making the decision to compete at the very public Paralympics was not easy. In time, she realized that through self-acceptance and determination, she could tackle her disability head on.

This decision paid off when she won two gold medals and a silver medal in Atlanta in 1996; and at Sydney in 2000, she won a silver and bronze medal. While the Sydney Paralympics were successful for Katrina, her competitive spirit still left her with a desire to win gold again. To do that, she needed to take conscious action and become a gold-level performer in every aspect of her life.

In the four years between the Sydney and Athens Paralympics, Katrina mastered the alchemy of performance with a clear focus on understanding her mindset, and the results speak for themselves. At Athens in 2004, she won another gold medal in the 400-metre sprint and set a new Paralympic record.

Today, Katrina's running career is in the past, but her passion for helping others perform at their best continues to be her greatest inspiration. Katrina is the founding Director of Silver 2 Gold High-Performance Solutions. As a professional speaker, she has impressed audiences at an international level. This includes speaking at the United Nations International Year of Sport in New York, 2006.

Due to her own experience in dealing with a disability and a desire to help others, Katrina is a passionate humanitarian. She currently organizes leadership treks to Nepal, including Everest Base Camp, and she raises funds for the health, education, and protection of children in Nepal.

"Stop looking for angels and start looking for angles. We must learn to persist and resist. Persist in your efforts. Resist giving in to distraction, discouragement, and disorder."

—RYAN HOLIDAY

THE POWER OF PRACTICAL RESILIENCE

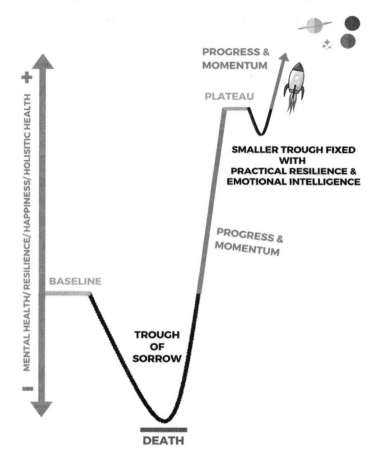

BECOMING SELF-AWARE AND SELF-ACCEPTING OF PITFALLS

To be able to recognize a setback and pull yourself out of it is a blessing. Years ago, I had dug myself so deep into a negative state of worrying and hating who I was that it felt like I was meters underground in a mine that was ready to collapse any minute. Nowadays, I may encounter a temporary pitfall, but I have the tools of Practical Resilience to get me out so I can shoot for that stratosphere again. You can't avoid pitfalls, but you can prevent the issue from becoming worse than what it actually is.

Understanding how to apply The Practical Resilience formula is crucial when shit hits the fan, because there's a dramatic increase in your emotional intelligence that recognizes what's going on. When you develop a state of reassurance, then it's okay to come across adversity again. Embrace the adversity and it will lead you toward great things at the most unexpected times.

WHEN SHIT HITS THE FAN

For those who can remember Robin Williams, he was a very iconic man who brought us so much joy with his comedic acting abilities. He was one of my childhood heroes, and watching him perform gave me a sense of warmth and had me genuinely on the floor laughing out loud. It wasn't only his humor that amazed me, but I was intrigued by the sheer creativity in his genius nature, especially as he played various roles in so many movies.

I remember Robin Williams' death very clearly. I was traveling in Montreal and having a great time with a bunch of friends—until we heard the news, and then everyone around me was in a very melancholic state. I'll be honest, I shed a few tears, and the only thing I could do was put on Jumanji and mourn the loss of a childhood hero.

I also remember another loss of a great person, Heath Ledger. He's from my generation, and was a master craftsman that everyone revered and respected. In fact, some thought he was a genius at what he did. Yet, we awoke to the news one morning that he had committed suicide, which was blamed on his infatuation with pre-scription medications.

Unfortunately, suicide took the best of both of these men. It doesn't make sense how two guys who seemed to have it all ended their lives in the worst way possible. Many people remembered MLK and Princess Diana, and when they died it stunned us.

The message I'm trying to get across is mental health is fucking real, especially with the examples of these two amazing men. In Australia alone, six people a day commit suicide, and the number of those struggling with anxiety and depression is rising by the minute. Nine times out of ten, we end up seeing a doctor when our headspace is out of whack and meds appear to be the only answer.

Whether it's Prozac, Xanax, or some drug we can't pronounce, it may be designed and created to stabilize the situation. However, when drugs are abused and taken for granted, it's probably going to make matters worse. We live in a society where everyone wants instant results and a quick-fix. When all these engineered chemicals are constantly injected into our body, other side effects take over and sometimes make matters worse. Billions of dollars are spent every year on medicinal drugs that are intended to address the mental health field, but are they being put to good use?

Like I said earlier in the book, if you're on medication already, I'm not telling you to stop taking your prescription medicine, because your doctor has more knowledge about your health profile. But for those who feel the need to see a doctor to get that quick-fix to cure their mental health struggles, especially for the first time, please really think this one through before taking any action. I want you to understand there's a safer, cheaper, and healthier way than the placebo of getting a drug to cure you. You don't need the symptoms that can cause psychological effects like meds did with me and with many others in this world. Yes, you have to build the foundation and take the time to do your own research, but you're worth it. You can focus on the Practical Resilience formula as well as the entirety of this book to help you get the support you need to make intelligent choices for your own health.

Famous celebrities might not make you realize how prevalent the mental health stigma is, but when it affects your friends and family, then you really need to take action and do your research.

RESPECTING OPINIONS

As you embark on this new journey, many people will be amazed at your transformation and progress, and they will support you. Yet, in the law of big numbers, you will always come across those who aren't a fan. We call them haters and naysayers.

When your brain is telling you to fight back, you shouldn't let those apprehensive thoughts get to you. Remember, your brain wants you to retaliate because it's functioning in survival mode against a nasty remark. You might have to respect the other person's opinion, but you don't have to believe it. You are in control of your thoughts and decisions, so why should their opinions matter? Certainly, they are not the expert in the field, which means you don't have to respond to their remarks.

Basically, you don't have to listen to everyone who has an opinion about your health. And don't overthink the situation or the remarks made to you. It might irritate the person making the nasty remark if you don't respond or give them an argument, but that's okay. Your values are evidently higher than theirs.

TWENTY-FIVE COGNITIVE BIASES THAT WE SUCCUMB TO

Have you ever wondered why people respond to celebrities differently than they do to regular people they know and interact with every day? That "limited time offer" will sell quicker, the industry believes, when a celebrity endorses the product. For example, have you ever wondered why a car salesman will offer you a free coffee when you visit the showroom, even if you're only planning to look around? It's because of cognitive biases.

A cognitive bias is a systematic error in our thinking that affects the decisions and judgments that people make. Often, these biases are related to memory. The way you remember an event may be biased for a number of reasons, which can lead to biased thinking and decision making.

There are twenty-five main cognitive biases we succumb to regarding the psychology of human misjudgment and why we act the way we do. If you've never heard of cognitive biases, it's your lucky day! Acknowledging these twenty-five tools WILL NOT ONLY strengthen your mental capacity and relationships, but you'll be much further ahead than everyone else playing this game of life.

Following is a list of the twenty-five main cognitive biases, how these tendencies affect the everyday person, and how you can use them to your advantage.

1. **REWARD AND PUNISHMENT SUPER-RE-SPONSE TENDENCY.** Bad behavior is intensely habit-forming when it's rewarded. People change their behavior and cognition for sex, friendship, companionship, advancement in status, and, of course, money. Do you remember Granny's Rule? "You must eat your carrots before you get dessert. You have to put in the hard work before you get the reward."

2. **LIKE/LOVING TENDENCY.** Men and women will devote themselves in a courtship competition for the affection and approval of someone not related to them. This cognitive bias tends to make people favor people, products, and actions merely associated with the object of their affection. This causes admiration, which can reverse the affects of being inversely proportional.

3. **DISLIKE/HATING TENDENCY.** Ignoring virtues is the object of dislike. This affects your behavior of a high moral standard. Unlike the Like/Loving Tendency, this tendency results in disliking people, products, and actions merely associated with an object of dislike and can distort other facts to encourage hatred. For example, hating Justin Bieber for whatever reason and disliking everyone associated with him. That's pretty much saying you're really not a fan of his music, even if he didn't do anything wrong to you. If he's eating a type of sandwich in an Instagram picture, that type of thinking can make you create such

cognitive dissonance that you hate that sandwich too. This is where you need to have empathy and look at the situation from their perspective and realize they are also human beings. Hey, they may not be perfect, but don't be that guy who has a problem with everyone and everything.

4. **DOUBT-AVOIDANCE TENDENCY.** The human brain is programmed with a tendency to quickly remove doubt by reacting to some decision. This cognitive bias is often triggered by a combination of puzzlement and stress. To get through this, do a mental pros vs. cons list.

5. **INCONSISTENCY-AVOIDANCE TENDENCY.** The brain conserves programming space by being reluctant to change. As Warren Buffett says, "Chains of habit are too light to be felt until they're too heavy to be broken." The rare life that is wisely lived has in it many good habits that are maintained, and then there are many bad habits that should be avoided or cured. It is much easier to prevent a habit from forming than to change it. This is where you should always be experimenting with what works well for you in the long run and doubling-down on those habits.

6. **CURIOSITY TENDENCY.** Culture greatly increases the effectiveness of curiosity in advancing knowledge; the curious are also provided with a lot of fun and wisdom long after a formal education has ended. The moral is to always remain curious, because asking

more questions will lead to the uncovering of the "unknown-unknowns," as mentioned in Chapter 2. When you tap into that area of your brain that promotes thoughts, you can discover more areas that lead to opportunities you haven't even thought possible.

7. **KANTIAN FAIRNESS.** As an obverse consequence of "fair-sharing" conduct, hostility is expected yet not provided. For example, feeling anger toward a stranger that you allowed to go before you through an intersection when he didn't have the courtesy to wave at you in return.

8. **ENVY/JEALOUSY TENDENCY.** Feeling and showing envious resentment toward someone for their achievements, possessions, or perceived advantages. Furthermore, a chance of displaying resentful suspicion that one's partner is attracted to or involved with someone else. This cognitive bias often triggers hatred and injury.

9. **RECIPROCATION TENDENCY.** The automatic tendency of humans to reciprocate both favors and disfavors has long been noticed as extreme. Reciprocation clearly facilitates group cooperation for the benefit of members; that is collaboration. But if someone purposely creates extreme and dangerous consequences for you, then don't expect anything in return, especially if I give something away that you bought me.

10. **INFLUENCE FROM MERE ASSOCIATION**

TENDENCY. Don't react to someone's past success. "Always tell us the bad news promptly, it's the good news that can wait." Look for dangerous aspects of the new relationship that were not present when past success occurred. When a championship sporting team wins a title one year and then thinks they have the secret and will win again the next year, they have a tendency not to improve their game, even though they were the best. The reason is that complacency takes over and that winning mentality is lost because it's too comfortable.

11. **SIMPLE, PAIN-AVOIDING PSYCHOLOGICAL DENIAL.** The reality is too painful to bear, so someone distorts the facts until they become bearable. This cognitive bias's most extreme outcomes are usually mixed up with love, death, and chemical dependency, including hard drugs and alcohol. You need to recognize what's going on so it doesn't result in becoming the bitch of your own brain.

12. **EXCESSIVE SELF-REGARD TENDENCY.** This is where you have to drop your ego because it's highly recommended that you shouldn't appear condescending. "Never underestimate the man who overestimates himself." In this case, stay humble yet truthful.

13. **OVER-OPTIMISM TENDENCY.** "What a man wishes, that also he will believe" (Demosthenes). The message here is don't be narcissistic. If I think my IQ is higher than it is, it potentially becomes a big problem.

Thinking that my IQ is lower than it actually is can be a good thing. So, stay humble because everyone benefits.

14. **DEPRIVAL SUPER REACTION TENDENCY.** Loss seems to hurt more than the gain seems to help, which results in a loss aversion. For example, if you feel pleasure from gaining ten dollars, you feel more displeasure when losing ten dollars. People react with irrational intensity to even a small loss or a threatened loss, whether it's property, love, friendship, dominated territory, opportunity, status, or anything else that you deem as valuable. You may win when you gamble, but if you haven't continued playing for the rest of the night, you might feel the odds are higher for losing than continuing to bet.

15. **SOCIAL-PROOF TENDENCY.** Complex behavior is simplified when you can automatically observe what's going on around you, and then act on your impulse. It's really a game of monkey-see, monkey-do. This cognitive bias is triggered in the presence of puzzlement or stress, and particularly when both exist. Learn how to ignore the examples from others when they're doing something wrong because, having only a few skills, you can learn more from turning away than following the crowd.

16. **CONTRAST-MISREACTION TENDENCY.** This tendency causes a disadvantage for customers who are buying merchandise and services. To make an ordinary price seem low, the vendor will very frequently

create a high artificial price that is much higher than the original price. Then, the store will advertise their standard price, which the customer views as a big reduction from the original price.

17. **STRESS-INFLUENCE TENDENCY.** Light stress can slightly improve performance, especially during examinations; heavy stress causes dysfunction. For instance, most people know that an acute stress depression makes a person have dysfunctional thinking, which then becomes a stress-misinfluence tendency because it can cause extreme pessimism.

18. **AVAILABILITY-MISWEIGHING TENDENCY.** Everyone's imperfect and has a limited-capacity brain that easily drifts into working with what's available to it. Therefore, the mind overweighs what is easily available. For example, if you're a college student, you might decide to major in the wrong things and minor in the right things. An idea or a fact is not worth more just because it's easily available to you. You know when there's junk food at eye level on the shelves at the supermarket, it's placed there to entice you to buy it, as opposed to putting that same junk food on the top shelf where no one sees it. That's because it's easier to tempt you to grab those items and put them in your shopping cart. The same is true when you're at home and looking for something to eat. You open your pantry door, and the tendency is to grab something that's at eye level rather than look for food

that's on the top or bottom shelf, because it requires less effort.

19. **USE-IT-OR-LOSE-IT TENDENCY.** You can lose your skills by not using them. But when you double-down on those skills that are useful to you, you can use them more often, which will help you push hard to achieve your goals in health, wealth, relationships, and happiness/gratitude. Be sure to constantly practice your skills on a daily basis so you don't get soft and forget them. If you're working out, your muscles will get sore if you stop and start your activities with too many days of no exercise.

20. **DRUG-MISINFLUENCE TENDENCY.** Everyone makes mistakes, but when you avoid the big mistakes and start telling yourself that heroin is vital, your brain is receiving bad information that could potentially harm you. We've all seen so much drug and alcohol abuse, but it's interesting how it will always cause a moral breakdown if there's any need. Usually it involves massive denial. When tempted to drink your sorrows away, or when getting absolutely hammered sounds like a great idea, just know that it will only make things worse, and it can make you look like an idiot.

21. **SENESCENCE-MISINFLUENCE TENDENCY.** With advanced age comes a natural cognitive decay, which is usually different among individuals and is dependent on the speed of its progression. Continuous

thinking and learning, done with joy, can somewhat help delay what is unavoidable. There will always be those older than you who will say, "I'm too old for this." Well, yeah, when you think like that, you're totally right. Michelangelo David said, "I am still learning." He was eighty-seven years old at the time, so why should he stop learning?

22. **AUTHORITY-MISINFLUENCE TENDENCY.** Human society is formally organized into dominance hierarchies with their culture augmenting the natural follow-the-leader tendency of man. This was derived from our ancestors. Just be careful who you appoint to have the power, because a dominant authority figure will often be hard to remove.

23. **TWADDLE TENDENCY.** People tend to spend a lot of time on meaningless activities that accomplish little or nothing. If you're in business, you must value the business in order to value the stock. Charlie Munger said, "The principle job of an academic administration is to keep the people who don't matter from interfering with the work of the people."

24. **REASON-RESPECTING TENDENCY.** Unfortunately, this cognitive bias is so strong that even a person's meaningless or incorrect reasons will increase compliance with their orders and requests. It's merely a conditioned reflex based on a widespread appreciation of the importance of reasons. For example, an executive jumping the line to use the printer

and explaining his reason (or giving an excuse) as to why everyone else in line needs to use it after him, because his work is more important.

25. **LOLLAPALOOZA EFFECT.** Getting extreme consequences from psychological tendencies that act in favor of a particular outcome. Simply, this is several cognitive biases working together at any given moment.

Charlie Munger, who is Warren Buffett's main business partner at Berkshire Hathaway, used a term in his book *Poor Charlie's Almanack* that meant when several cognitive biases are used in one setting, it creates a dynamic known as the Lollapalooza Effect. You'll notice it's number twenty-five on the list, but I've elaborated further on this one as it deserves its own section regarding the reasoning of how powerfully it can impact us.

HERE'S AN EXAMPLE WHERE THE LOLLAPALOOZA EFFECT WORKS IN A NEGATIVE STATE

OPEN-OUTCRY AUCTIONS. This one is dangerous purely because the auctioneer is literally above you, so that represents an authority tendency (#22), then there's social proof (#15) in play, and the other bidders are placing higher bets that create a reciprocating effect (#9) to battle and one-up the other person. And because the item will go to the winner, there's a feeling of loss-aversion if you truly want the prize, which relates to a deprival-super reaction tendency (#14). Not to mention, the starting bid may even begin as something quite ridiculous so it'll just increase the chances of attracting more bidders, and thus creating a contrast-misreaction (#16). This style of auction is designed to manipulate people into idiotic behavior. Simply, don't go to such auctions.

HERE'S AN EXAMPLE WHERE THE LOLLAPALOOZA EFFECT WORKS IN A POSITIVE STATE

RUNNING COMMUNITY. Becoming part of any sporting community has a tenfold (at least) affect because of all the neurobiological and psychological benefits. Firstly, you're joining a movement with others who may be on the same path. They most likely think how you do (#2), reducing stress (#17) to a bearable level. Then it becomes the catalyst to be an escapism, a type of therapy per se that is much safer than chemical dependency (#11). This will create such a mindset of curiosity (#6) so as to gain an active and healthier lifestyle, both mentally and physically, that results in an exponential return. It may even influence others with your story and progress to be a part of the movement. Later it generates social proof (#15) to empower others to strive where they didn't think it was possible for them. I know from my experience that I always have a goal in mind that ensures I'm staying well-disciplined, or else I may succumb to relaxing for too long and losing where I am (#19).

WHAT IT MEANS IF YOU'RE SELF-AWARE AND SELF-ACCEPTANT OF WHO YOU ARE

If you can recognize the emotions you're facing and undergoing, it will prevent you from retaliating because that's what your survival brain wants. Know that when we build this foundation in us, not only is it inevitable in growing emotional intelligence, but we're agreeing on the fact that we aren't perfect, nor is anyone else. The house isn't going to crumble (and that house is us) because we're much more secure in the person we have become, despite our messed-up past.

CHAPTER 5

───

RIDING THAT NOTION OF EMOTION

"The compression between the soles of my ragged joggers and the light grey smooth pavement has my feet in pain from constant pounding through such a sensation. My focus on foot placement is that much of a priority. I honestly have no idea what else has been on my mind these past few hours. The town could have been up in flames, and I wouldn't have even noticed. My focus is on where I'm running and that's all I care about right now." —May 12, 2015

What actually motivates a person to take on a new goal? No, it's not a quote slapped onto a backdrop you saw on an Instagram photo. There's a science behind why we have *drive*. It comes down to the Four M's of Motivation.

1. **MATERIALS.** Objects or money that matter. Examples: Floyd Mayweather and Conor McGregor.
2. **MASTERY.** Becoming renowned at a skill. Examples: Michael Jordan and Michael Phelps.
3. **MATING (FRIENDSHIP).** Building concrete relationships and growing their social circles. Examples: James Corden and Casanova.
4. **MOMENTUM.** How movements are created that cultivate inspiration and thought-leadership. Examples: Elon Musk and Arnold Schwarzenegger.

We're all different but have tendencies for all four. However, you'll have a primary "M" motive, then a secondary, and then the other two won't be as dominant. For me, I'm not very materialistic and I'm not aiming to be the best or quickest endurance athlete. Personally, I'm momentum-based followed by mating, since I've always been a person who loves people and is fascinated with human behavior and social dynamics.

Literally, I get called the word *crazy* more times than my name, and I'm not even joking. The thing is that I don't think I'm crazy. Sure, taking part in absurd and obscure events could baffle a person who wonders why I would do that. However, to me, what's crazy is wasting your time by not focusing on your dreams and by complaining how shitty your life is. Consider all that wasted time that you spent investing in things that didn't help your situation, like binge-watching a series on Netflix. We have the same twenty-four hours in a day as Elon Musk and Bill Gates, but then why are they incredibly successful? Because they deployed and invested their energy into the right things, that's why. Neither of them were brought up rich.

However, there are crazier people than me. A prime example is Pete Kostelnick. Pete is an ultrarunner based out of Lincoln, Nebraska, in the United States. He holds multiple records including the fastest course track on Badwater 135 (the world's toughest foot race), and he recently broke the Guinness World Record for fastest time across the USA on foot. The previous record was forty-six days, but Pete smashed the 3,100 mile distance in a whopping forty-two days, six hours, and thirty minutes! Now, that's crazy!

Everyone always says, "Follow your passion." I'm going to call BS on that statement. It's fine if you know what you're already doing has a purpose and you enjoy every second of it. Otherwise, when you're in that state of mind and thinking, "What am I doing with my life?" then perhaps you should forget about doing what you love. The saying should be tweaked to say, "**Follow your curiosity.**"

The problem is that once you find something you love and it feels like work, then you might not love it anymore. So, you need to find something you like, not love.

It can be the greatest feeling when you believe you've found your calling. But the point is that you need to pursue something you enjoy so your life seems much more exciting, instead of doing something just to pay the bills. Honestly, that is always a thought at the back of the mind. This is where you have to be careful when making this passion something you want for the rest of your life.

"I have no special talents. I am only passionately curious."

—ALBERT EINSTEIN

At the end of the day, what it all comes down to is curiosity. If you're still interested and curious in what you're doing even after the pitfalls, the tough days, and bad experiences, then you're in the right field. There's a great book on the topic that I've read called *Curious* by Ian Leslie. Highly recommend this one on your bookshelf!

As I keep pushing myself and pursuing this endurance adventure, the curiosity is still there. Here's a little caveat for you: I was never a runner to begin with. Especially at school, I hated the sport. It came to a point in my life when I was so desperate to get out of that rabbit hole that running didn't seem as bad as I perceived it in my teens. Once I finished my first marathon, I automatically wanted to know how far I could push my body. This was a great goal, scary enough to make me grow. But once I realized I enjoyed running and was able to push through the adversarial moments and mental mind games throughout training and events, I developed a passion. I'm constantly thinking about how I can do better, raising my own bar, and learning from the best. Yet, the passion would not be there if I wasn't still very curious to see what could be achieved. Instead, it's grown on me to tackle more challenges that would test my limits.

A great example of someone who followed what they love instead of what they like is Michael Jordan, the GOAT (Greatest Of All Time) of basketball. MJ retired from professional basketball after the Chicago Bulls won their first three-peat. He decided to leave the court and take up baseball because he absolutely loved the sport when he was a kid. But we all know how that panned out. He wasn't the greatest player, and he wasn't built to play baseball, no matter how much he loved the sport. If he hadn't retired from basketball, then he could've won a few more championships with the Bulls. But hey, who am I to judge MJ? The man was a weapon on the court. He knew the game better than anyone else because he was a learning machine and just wanted to get better and win.

HOW CURIOSITY CAN MAKE THIS WORLD A BETTER PLACE

Speaking of curiosity, I'm reminded of the story of a dear friend of mine, Peter Watkins. Peter is what I'd call an "Altruistic Capitalist" who's no stranger to the investing and financial world. But he's not your typical VC. He's more of a Robin Hood, if anything. He is incredibly self-less where many others are greedy. That's how he came to care about charity giving, which is quite fascinating.

Quoting nonchalantly, "I believe that I am a fortunate man," he always knew that when he learned the answer to, "Why am I here?" he would follow his destiny. This concept is beautifully described in his favorite novel, *The Alchemist* by Paolo Coelho.

When you honor your personal legend, life is simple. You do whatever you have to do so you can sleep well. Being true to yourself allows that to happen. Behaving in this manner also protects you from the opinions of others. Knowing Peter, he doesn't feel the need to ask anyone if he is doing the right thing. Peter understands we are all a product of our environment. We behave the same way as the five people we spend the most time with, and we base our view of the world on a myriad of different variances. Therefore, if we are true to ourselves, we are less affected by outside influences.

Many years ago, Peter took a year off with pay and traveled the world. During those twelve months, he had many adventures. One of the first things he did (in Louisville, Kentucky) was appear on television as a guest. Because he was born in the UK, living in Australia, and traveling the world, the host felt he would be an interesting person to interview. At the conclusion of the thirty-minute interview, Peter was asked what advice he had for the viewers. The reply was not about giving advice, but more a set of observations, per se. Paraphrasing Peter:

> I've observed that the least comfortable place is merely a "comfort zone." Settling for less than you deserve is not a good place for anyone who has stretched themselves. It is true that when you experience what can be, it is unsettling when you go back to your normal life because it's not what calms your soul.
>
> When you listen to your heart, life will be challenging. You have to be able to laugh at whatever situation you create for yourself. Be kind to people and they will reciprocate. This is important because you will often need the kindness of others while you follow your dream. It's important to focus on what you must do

to achieve peace of mind. The very act of continuing to march in the direction you have mapped out for yourself will sustain you through difficult times. You will have many of them, but it will be hard to concentrate on working for someone else and giving them value when your mind is somewhere else.

On a personal level, a relationship will be challenging when you are not capable of making your partner the most important driving force in your life. Speaking from experience, to give up the person you love to follow your magnificent obsession will test you every day. If you have children, it becomes even more difficult. So, if you truly believe there is a reason you're here, and being true to that reason is more important than anything else in your life, the people you love will respect your decision. In that way, it becomes simpler for you to pursue your dream.

Believe you are where you are meant to be, doing what you are meant to do and knowing you are guided to arrive where you are needed. "I know why I do what I do. It's because the people I need to manifest my vision will appear when I am ready." Though how it will be done becomes evident after I've had more learning experiences. Faith of some sort will allow me to advance in the direction of my dreams. I know I will be successful. If I never give up, I do not have to ask if I failed. With the really big questions ahead of you, only your answers matter.

Celebrate your successes, give yourself praise, and do not wait for someone else to show up in case they do not arrive. There is a hero in all of us. May you find the hero in you.

Peter was unimaginably curious. It's as if it's a non-negotiable trait we should all have. It keeps us functioning and steered away from boredom and complacency.

PRACTICAL TIPS YOU CAN USE TO SPARK THE CURIOSITY INSIDE OF YOU

- Pursue a career you like, so you're not stuck in a job you hate.
- Be open-minded. Get rid of any black-and-white thinking where you believe that something hasn't been done right or doesn't conform to your standards. The quicker you get rid of this style of philosophy, the quicker you'll become more creative.
- Take up hobbies you would never dream of doing or that aren't in your comfort zone.
- Don't be afraid to ask "why" about anything you're unsure of. Continuing to ask "why" can actually get to the root cause of an issue.
- Read a broad range of books. For example, get a book on philosophy, history, sports, business, finance, psychology, love, biographies, etc. You don't have to read the entire book. Even one snippet of knowledge can create the driving force that has you researching a specific topic. My room has been transformed from a man cave to a library—a hub of knowledge to drown myself in, as opposed to the heavy illicit substances and hard liquor that used to be the antidote.

Regarding the last point on books, on average, a CEO will read fifty-two books in one year, which is usually one book a week. He knows he can't learn everything himself, so he listens to the experts in various fields so he can fast-track his own journey. Now, reading a book can take some time. It may even take longer than a week to read some books.

But here's the kicker. You don't need to read the entire book. Each book usually has that one golden nugget, which is primarily what the book is about. The rest is filled with stories, and whatever the author decides. I've found a tool that I believe is a life hack, because it's allowed me to be on target to read more than fifty-two books in one year. It's an app called Blinkist. Every day you get a free book to read, and they summarize the entire thing in fifteen minutes via audio or an e-read.

This helpful app will save you hours!

INCREASE YOUR CURIOSITY TO SIMULATE AND IMAGINE THE FUTURE

Have you ever wondered how high-profile athletes are able to win gold medals? Some call it a winner's mentality, when in fact, they've visualized themselves winning it every possible chance they can. It's the narrative they're repeating in their head that brings them the success. For me, the story I repeat in my head goes like this, "I've got this, bro!" When I come across a tough challenge, I repeat my saying, which helps me finish my endurance tasks and allows me to face adversity head on.

Winning comes back to the perspective that's in your mind. I know I've dealt with many other tough times, so when I'm in the zone of running 160 km, then I'm in the right mindset.

DEADLINE HACKING

To really reduce the friction with decision making, we must act on each task without procrastinating and putting it off to the side. Sometimes the task we're working on is a predecessor activity, which means we can't move forward until it's done. If it's a task we've been anticipating and trying to avoid, then it simply means we have to go at it from a different angle. That is, via chunking and applying short deadlines with rewards.

The issue with procrastination (getting distracted and shying away from the task with something else) is we push the workload higher until we feel it's unachievable and couldn't be bothered anymore. Then all curiosity is gone, all because you were too focused on that YouTube channel showing cute cat videos. Trust me, I've been down that rabbit hole before.

If you were given a task at work and have been told to complete it by the end of the week, then you'll take your time with it. However, if the boss has noted that it must be done in the next three hours (especially if there's some reward), you'll get your ass into gear and finish that task before the three-hour deadline.

The trick for completing a task is to apply a relatively short deadline because it'll reduce over-thinking and you'll be nimble with getting the job done. You'll enter a state of thought-provoking focus on the major things that need to be completed. It can be a little stressful, but according to the cognitive bias stress-influence a little stress is healthy, while too much will make you become dysfunctional. So, set tight deadlines that are realistic yet maintain your high standards for quality.

To make sure you adhere to these deadlines, reward yourself even if it means checking your phone for a minute or two or grabbing a quick coffee. There's an effective app called Pomodoro that segments your task into thirty-minute intervals: twenty-five minutes of working on the task with five minutes of leisure. There's something about a countdown timer that has us completing that task on time.

Yes, this stuff can be hard, but remember your "why," which is the reason you took the task. Maybe you chose the task so you could feel more in control of your life or you wanted to prove you're worth more than the average worker. As much as the end result is an achievement, you should enjoy the process and make good progress along the way.

Here, optimism is key. Even with all the losses, I'm appreciative because I'll always know they're just minor setbacks. This validates that it didn't work so I know for next time that it wasn't as effective. Feedback from an experiment that didn't go as planned gives you more knowledge, as opposed to a failure that seems to take control of you.

Fear is a four-letter word that scares people into not trying anything. They don't even bother doing something due to their own fear. That's a realization why their lives are shit and boring. Are you one of those people? If so, sorry to say this, but you are the bitch of your own brain.

Now let's do something about it.

CHAPTER 6

MOMENTUM

GO SO FAST YOU'RE BREAKING THINGS

"It's currently 11:03 p.m. on this brisk winter night, and as I journal this gratifying moment of realization, I'm probably in the happiest and healthiest state I've been in for a long time. Goosebumps are riddled throughout my body as I write this. My health is on point with the amount of cardio I've put my body through during the last four months with training for my first marathon. I never understood the reason why people would pay for a race that involves torture and bring in an ambience of relief. It makes sense now. Ironically, we're running from our demons. I can see myself finishing my first marathon with flying colors." —June 19, 2015

Getting started is the first part, maintaining the rhythm is the next. To get off the couch after years of sedentary laziness is actually harder than running your first marathon, believe it or not. Your body is not used to the sudden abrupt transition (even if you used to be fit) when you've be rusty beyond relief. Shifting inertia to get the ball rolling is your first task and the beginning of creating a new habit. A good motivator to this new process is through small wins, because we all know how gratifying it is to feel triumphant. Once you have that slight taste of victory, it's viscerally hopeful.

"One day" becomes "day one."

With the set of ever-growing dominos, the smallest domino will not knock over the last piece in one hit; it's physically impossible. The only way the last domino will be knocked over is if all the other pieces beforehand are knocked over in sequence. Metaphorically speaking, to reach your vision in life, start small with what you can do today and get that last win over time through growing by incremental and exponential change. It's like all the endurance events I've done, I didn't start out with a 160 km run straightaway. I started with a killer-driven mindset to tackle a 10 km (6 mi.) run, then a marathon, followed by a 50 km (31 mile) run, which subsequently became a habit for running longer distances. Because I had built up a crescendo of progress, I could tackle that 160 km run more than once in a short time.

To get things rolling, you have to do what you can to prevent the ball from stopping. Why? Because a habit can easily be broken if you give it a break for too long. Why do you think we put weight back on after we stop those twelve-week diet programs? We go back to how we used to be. Note, nothing against the twelve-week programs in any field, but if you don't continue the work afterward, then you're heading straight back to square one. Therefore, be quick and nimble; speed trumps everything, and it's a great proponent of progress and feedback. Now, your journey becomes quantifiable and measurable for growth.

This may sound great and all, but it won't mean anything if you don't have the endgame in mind. Goal setting is highly crucial in this process, because it will make you accountable!

ACCOUNTABILITY WILL PROTECT YOU FROM YOURSELF

Profound, hey? But how are you meant to make yourself accountable without anything to put it toward? That's when you implement goal setting; something about structure and a tight deadline will get your ass into gear for quick results. Goals are a great tool, but I've learned from experience that when you set too many goals at a time, it can cripple you. Focus on three to five goals at a time to set a good rhythm and so you won't feel burned out. This is achievable by only having a small handful of goals to work with at any given time.

As the progress gains momentum, so does your confidence. This will give you the urge to strive for greatness. Yes, we most definitely have to aim big and set high standards to get to the level where execution happens so easily. Even the tasks that seem impossible must start small.

YOUR AIM IS TO IMPROVE MULTIPLE PILLARS IN LIFE—TAKE JOHN'S EXAMPLE

John is a thirty-four-year-old accountant who works too much with numbers and is dying to have a career change in a field he cares about. Because of his marriage breakup from two years ago, John is 30 kg (66 lb.) overweight, struggling with self-confidence, and is heavily depressed. But where he finds a sense of inner peace is through photography. He can easily focus on this eighteen hours a day. Time flies when you're doing something you love.

With John's situation, he has three areas he could improve. Let's look at his goals.

1. **HEALTH FOCUSED.** He wants to lose 7 kg (15 lb.) in three months.
2. **SIDE PROJECT FOCUSED.** He wants to use photography to document his weight loss journey. Alongside driving out to a new location every weekend or when he's not working too far away, his side project gets him out of the house and using his craft to focus on taking epic photos in each location.
3. **GRATITUDE FOCUSED.** He wants to document his journey on social media that lists his results so he can inspire others. He's coming to the realization that he's making an impact.

This may sound like a great deal to tackle, but it really isn't. Looking after his health will not only reduce his weight problem but automatically give him self-confidence when he starts to lose the weight. His goal is to lose 7 kg instead of the full 30 kg at the beginning of this journey. Once he starts losing the weight, his happiness will start to show and he will be on the road to greatness! Working on his passion will give him a sense of self-compassion by getting in touch with something intrinsic. This will be one step closer to putting a smile on his face. Depression is a state of mind. It can be changed in an instant. If you think the world is shitty, then it is. It's the same if you think the world is great. What we perceive is the outlook and the attitude. Getting a sense of happiness in John's scenario will change his fixed belief that he's not worthless. A paradigm shift, per se.

By getting out of the house and take photos outside, John will be functioning outside of his comfort zone. He will be in touch with nature, realizing there's more to life than being cooped up in a house with an abundance of snacks and a TV screen at his fingertips.

The key for John is to listen only to 1 percent of the experts. He needs to lose weight and he wants to gain the courage to see a personal trainer at his local gym on a weekly basis. Working out this way will make the PT's life easier when he tells him his situation and the amount he wants to lose. Coaches/strategists/trainers need to know the end goal before they can implement a plan. Otherwise, they'll ask you, "What do you want to achieve?" and if you say, "I don't know," then you're wasting their time.

Have you also noticed how each of these solutions in three different fields are integrated with each other? Once John is able to reach those milestones, his next goals will easily transition into the following:

4. **HEALTH FOCUSED.** He wants to lose another 7kg in three months and he's now halfway to the total 30 kg end goal.

5. **SIDE HUSTLE FOCUSED.** In the previous three months, John had gained some momentum with plenty of photography so he was able to focus on his craft and understand more of the technical details. Throughout social media, there are others on the same path or those fascinated with his progress. He has now become a conduit to start taking photos for other people because of his skill and expertise. At first, he may take on free work to grow his name and build the rapport with his fan base, but after enough pro bono work, he may get recommended via word of mouth and have the ability to get paid, even if it's only a small income. Whereas goal #2 was side project focused, because there's an income involved, it's now side hustle focused.

At least it's a sign he can get paid for his hustle with high curiosity. Obviously, John has a long way to go, but there's momentum behind it all. There's plenty of demand in his craft and by focusing on making it a goal, he could quit his crappy accounting job and make this his full-time gig. However, he must hustle during every spare moment when there's a full-time job in a different profession to pay the bills, but it's only temporary. How long? Well, it depends how hungry John is.

6. **GRATITUDE FOCUSED.** In the three months of gaining some traction on social media with his weight loss, John was able to demonstrate that his results speak for his actions. Becoming an impact with those also on a similar progression, John's following may be small, but it's slowly growing each day. This makes him want to share it more with others. Inspired with other fitness journeys, he has an epiphany, and pictures himself at the finish line of a 7 km Spartan Race obstacle course that can really test him. Yes, this is a scary moment for John, but he knows how far he's come, and part of him wants to really give back. John has several friends in the army and some have PTSD. So, he decides to dedicate his time and raise $500 for the Wounded Warriors cause. Now, fundraising is an added element, but with the power of his growing social media presence and his emotional connection behind the cause, he makes it happen. This extra effort will drive him to finish the race and experience gratitude at a whole new level.

7. **RELATIONSHIP FOCUSED.** Over the years, John has been lonely with both his social circles and intimate relationships. By throwing himself into this transition to look after his health, it's transformed this isolated, sad man into one who's meeting other people who are now becoming close friends. Where it was scary at first, it's now not so scary since he's gained friends in both the field of photography and

training. John has even been introduced to several women throughout his journey and it's increasing his self-confidence.

See how John started with three or four simple tasks that were easily achieved and quantified for progress? By having goals to work with that are integrated makes his life easier. He now knows he will be able to reach that end goal. It will take some time, but it's all part of the process.

GOING STRAIGHT TO THE TOP

Over the past few years, I've been asking ultrarunners from all corners of the globe what they do to train for these monstrous runs. There were no straight answers because everyone has their own style.

With all this democratic thinking, it's best to go straight to the top and learn from someone prolific in the field. Dean Karnazes, who's a famous ultrarunner who ran fifty marathons in fifty consecutive days in fifty different states of America, mentioned in his book, *50 Marathons 50 Days: The Secrets to Super Endurance*, that he recommends going on a long trek initially. It doesn't matter whether it's hiking, jogging, or walking, he suggests just doing it for an entire day in any direction as a way to mentally prepare yourself for an ultramarathon.

It's rare in our modern society to spend an entire day outside, and there's just something enchanting about watching a day go by from the exterior of a building, rather than locked inside.

It's not just in health where it's important to go straight to the top, it also applies to business, relationships, and any facet of life that requires growth. Would you rather get your love-life advice from a person who has been through several divorces, or seek advice and insight from a couple who has been together for fifty-plus years and their love is stronger than ever? I hope you picked the latter.

DOUBLING-DOWN ON WHAT'S WORKING

Initially, I embraced running on a larger scale as it was obvious for my need to get fit, both mentally and physically. The running also got me in the right mindset. Then I thought, "Maybe this is the year I should train for my first marathon." That, in itself, is a milestone for anyone who hadn't done one already! By the end of 2015, I had completed eight events ranging from a 10 km fun run to a 42 km marathon.

Since starting this journey, my life has changed dramatically, especially in the last few years, all for the greater good. I've gone from partying most weekends to training most days. I wouldn't have it any other way, because it's given me ten-times the return on my health.

Like the saying "double-down on what's working," that's exactly what I've been doing. If anything, I've been tripling-down or going all-in because I have a visceral hope that my I have that winning hand in poker where I'll finish off the Royal Flush, and it'd be stupid to not go all-in. At first, I was willing to compete in one event a month, but after pushing myself to see what I was capable of, I completed forty events in 2016!

Believe it or not, running has easily given me at least a tenfold return on investment. Investments don't always have to be money related. You can be doing something to give yourself a better future return, whether it's regarding your family, health, or even your social life.

FOLLOWING IS A LIST OF REASONS WHY I CONTINUED THIS RUNNING LIFESTYLE

FEELING FITTER THAN EVER: Before I started running, I was 13.5 kg heavier. My body has become pretty lean from all the cardio, which means it makes sense to keep on going so I don't resort to gaining all that weight back.

COMPLIMENTS: After running for almost three years, my friends and even strangers will come up to me and tell me how lean and slim I look. After multiple years of constant partying, all this cardio has shaped my body into a lean machine. It does feel awesome being known as a person who is always running for a cause greater than himself.

STRENGTHENING THE MIND AND BODY: Little did I realize that an abundance of running would not only change my body into one I've always dreamt of having, but it has transformed my mind into becoming incredibly versatile and able to handle stress on the fly. When you run, you're training your lungs to keep pushing so you can finish the race, profoundly. This has taught me to apply the same to everyday adversity, and I've learned to deal with problems head-on instead of running away from them.

PROLONGING MY HEALTH: Because I'm still in my twenties and taking this fitness venture on at a young age, I can continue doing this for many years and decades to maintain being fit. The last thing I'd want would be to get to my forties and wish I wasn't overweight or have trouble with any movement. It seems that running is one of only a few sports where the older generation will kill it more than the younger generation. Why? It's because they know their body and the mind game better than anyone else. Some are always keeping up or passing me on a few races.

MONEY: When I was partying every weekend or almost every day during my travels, a fair chunk of the funds would go toward booze and other illicit substances. So, spending my money on race entries and any essential extras is easily worth the switch. I have spent thousands of dollars on races, and at least I know it's been money well spent.

GROWING STRONGER AS FRIENDS: The amazing people I've met and still constantly meet have become such great friends, they're like a second family. It's always great to have a phone book of contacts who are always keen to join me for a mountain climb or a run on the trails.

BEING KNOWN IN THE RUNNING COMMUNITY: I have already completed close to sixty events to date, and after each one, I seem to be getting more recognized as the races go on. It's been great meeting new people and creating new friendships with other runners who love the sport and adventure as much as I do.

SENSE OF PURPOSE: As well as running to stay fit, running for a cause has been a pretty big eye-opener for bringing the feeling of gratitude to a whole new level. Being heavily involved with a venture like this, where you put your heart and energy into something that will help a great deal of people, helps you wake up each morning.

WHAT'S THE COMPONENT THAT MAKES A STARTUP OR PROJECT GREAT? MOMENTUM.

Getting it started is one thing, but growing quickly and

sustaining momentum is another. Just moving forward is crucial. If you're going in the wrong direction, then it's a waste of time. This resonates with the famous quote from Martin Luther King Jr:

"If you can't fly, then run. If you can't run, then walk. If you can't walk, then crawl. But whatever you do, you have to keep moving forward."

MEGHAN JARVIS, A DEAR FRIEND OF MINE

This is someone who has gone through trials and tribulations throughout her career as a professional athlete and female entrepreneur in business. She knows how to deal with diversity.

In her younger days, Meghan was a professional BMX racer and the true definition of a tomboy. She had short hair, wore baggy clothes, and didn't fit into the box of the female norm in Canada. Classmates ridiculed her, and it was difficult for her to make female friends due to her divergence into the masculine role as a BMX rider and extreme sports junkie.

Thanks to Meghan's environment and her parent's support, she kept pushing through the rejection from schoolmates and the outside world. She looked and acted different than most females her age. Through this period of life, Meghan became an extremely strong and independent young girl who had a self-belief that took her to the top of her sport with a top-three world ranking, and she even became a Ninja Warrior!

This confidence carried into the business world, where Meghan found herself surrounded by men while running a national and now global health and fitness app. It has assisted her to be confident as a female leader and she realized the power of overcoming diversity. After knowing Meghan for some time now, I can see she is extremely grateful for all the experiences she's had. They taught her to keep pushing ahead, no matter how difficult things got, or how alone she felt. She knew there was a light at the end of the tunnel.

FROM FEELING WORTHLESS TO WORTHY

You could say my momentum has accelerated exponentially since when I started running in early 2015. It's astounding how it exploded out of nowhere. From running in a handful of events in 2015 to almost sixty in such a short space is quite a leap!

Where did all this momentum come from? I got really curious with running, but running for charity also really pushed my body to run absurd races, and I wanted to reach fundraising goals. I actually enjoy these long-distance races. I'd much rather run an ultra over the conventional 42 km marathon. When the people I look up to are running 100-plus km endurance events, then it flips a switch in my head to be on that level.

With this much momentum, it's obvious that I will keep it going for the ongoing years. But never in a million years did I ever expect to go from running a regular road marathon to an ultramarathon on Mt. Everest.

MY RECENT EVEREST EXPERIENCE

Literally, I had the opportunity to run the world's highest ultramarathon on the infamous Mt. Everest, as well as summiting a 6,188 m glacial peak the week before. If you've run a marathon (or ultramarathon), you know it's a tough gig. You spend hours on your feet and all pistons are firing, especially in the mental regions. But having to do a race at very high altitude is another kettle of fish. And trust me, this fish can kill you. It managed to get one of the marathoners before the race even started.

Surely, there's some reason for taking on these two absurd events. The reason behind all this was to raise funds for Cystic Fibrosis, because the high altitude is in direct correlation with a CF patient having trouble breathing. What's it like running at high altitude exactly or having CF for that matter? Imagine breathing through a straw for hours (or days) on end.

Besides the restricted 9 percent oxygen (as opposed to an average 21 percent at sea level), this is one of the toughest races to take on, simply because it takes two weeks to get to the start line. Sounds simple, but anything can happen in that two-week period. If the weather goes wrong or if anyone on the team isn't acclimating properly, it can throw everything out of whack. It doesn't help when the air gets thinner as the days go by. I can tell you from my own experience, it quickly affects everyone's moods too.

The journey of the Island Peak climb and ultramarathon started from the capital of Nepal, Kathmandu. For what is a mad house full of shop hustlers, monkey temples, and international trekkers, this is where our team met up at the beautiful Hotel Shanker prior to our three-week adventure. The Tenzing Hillary Everest Marathon (THEM) is an iconic annual event in Nepal that commemorates the first successful ascent of Sir Edmund Hillary and Tenzing Norgay Sherpa on May 29, 1953.

The THEM added a 60 km ultramarathon into the series a few years back, and they recently gave racers an option to summit Island Peak, which is a nearby mountain in the Khumbu region.

Having no idea what I had signed myself up for, there was a positive indication that I'd be in good hands after meeting with my team in Kathmandu. There were only six of us climbers in the entire marathon group and six people is the perfect amount to ensure the team got the most value. If any more people had signed up, it could have been a little stressful to manage.

Fast forward a couple weeks and we were returning to Island Peak Base Camp. Our entire team was just exhausted after a fifteen-hour day. I went straight into the sleeping bag and got a solid ten-hour sleep. I needed the rest since we had to get ready for another week of trekking to Everest Base Camp (EBC) at extremely high altitude. It was all worth it to see the epic views from the top, not to mention we were one of the only few teams in history to have a 100 percent successful Island Peak summit. Not one of us pulled out or died. What a fucking relief.

There are many symptoms of high altitude sickness and a common one is a lack of appetite. A little frightened with my debacle earlier in the day, collapsing twice on the descent made me slightly worried for how I'd pull up the next day. I was concerned whether I'd be okay to continue (even if I forced myself to). Thankfully, after an extended sleep, I was as good as gold, and more importantly, hungry as hell.

We were only a couple stops away from EBC and the team was extremely eager to see the start line. It all seemed like smooth sailing to get to the Island Peak summit. A gradual walk up to Lobuche (16,200ft) from Dingboche (14,470ft) was a walk in the park. It may have been for the team, but that's when we noticed something quite odd.

Arriving in Thukla (15,950ft) for lunch at midday didn't feel necessary, but a little break wouldn't hurt. Heading into lunch and passing several zombie-like trekkers, (the high altitude can get the best of you when you're hypoxic and struggling to breathe), one woman we noticed was forced to go back to Dingboche to re-acclimate. If you're not feeling well from the high altitude, it's very highly recommended to get yourself to a lower altitude as quickly as possible. You're instructed to stay in that area for a *rest day*, as the body will increase in oxygen.

While that woman went down, another semiconscious

one continued to go higher. Our trek to Lobuche from Thukla was a crazy one. We arrived at the lodge early and explored the nearest glacier from a nearby hike and the Everest memorial, which is an area to commemorate the lives of climbers and Sherpas who hadn't made it back. It's an incredibly moving place to visit. After two weeks of constant trekking, it was starting to pay off, and EBC was merely a few kilometers away. The notable yellow tents were in view.

Dinner time changed its dynamic after a series of events. I'm not sure if it was the change of drastic weather earlier in the day, but at around 8:00 p.m., the woman I mentioned earlier, who had continued to trek when she shouldn't, finally arrived at our lodge. She looked terrible. She was escorted to the dining room and seated in front of the fire. She was wheezing for air and looked as if she was heavily intoxicated.

Word had it that she had suffered from HAPE (High Altitude Pulmonary Edema). That's when liquid leaks into the lungs and you need to get to a lower altitude, fast. Unfortunately, the walls at this lodge were paper thin, and we could clearly hear everything from those in adjacent rooms. One of the conversations I overheard was someone saying that a helicopter took a struggling marathoner back down to Namche Bazar at a tamer 5,375 km above sea level.

By 6:00 the next morning, I heard lots of noises and

phones ringing. What was initially loud chatter drastically changed into screaming for someone to get oxygen. Then I heard someone crying, "She's not breathing!"

I could hear everything happening. I won't disclose the runner's name or details, but she was a sky runner (mountain runner) who was heading to the infamous Ultra Trail Mont Blanc (UTMB) after this Everest race. UTMB is a widely famous 165 km ultramarathon in the mountains that spans three European countries; the trip requires exclusive qualifications to even get entry.

This runner's experience with high altitude was nothing short of new. The theory was she rushed it. She didn't observe the requirement for rest days to let her body acclimate as she climbed her way up. The people she was with mentioned that since she had done such a great deal of mountain running, it was hard to diagnose her.

The medic she was with had checked on her multiple times during the night before she died, and could see her snoring, which was a good sign that she was still alive. But by 6:00 a.m., it was too late to do much more for her.

Approaching EBC, the other teams were on edge and grumpy from living and struggling for air and lack of breath. It not only affected them physically, but I noticed that it affected a few people psychologically.

When there's news that one of the marathoners passed away during the trek, it creates a very emotional setting, which is a complete change in the group dynamic.

When a moment like this comes, certain thoughts and self-doubt are magnified in every racer's head, so much so that it's sometimes all they can think about for the next few days. A few racers were choppered out and taken to a lower altitude. Others simply trekked back down to Dingboche to downgrade to a half-marathon instead. The only way to continue the marathon was to push through and realize what we were there for—the reason "why." For me, it was to run for people with CF.

During the next two weeks, we had the most amazing clear weather, and it actually put us a day ahead of schedule to reach Base Camp. But the weather during any trek in the Nepali Khumbu region can be a hit or miss. The first night we were meant to stay at EBC, it snowed hard. That meant our chances were slim for seeing an amazing view of all the peaks at Kalapathar.

With my skewed logic that it would be an entire downhill race, I later found out that I'd be far from correct with this particular presumption. Starting at 5,360 m and ending at Namche Bazar at 3,400 m seemed like it would be a gradual declining run, but that all changed when the marathon and ultramarathon separated paths.

Going uphill in a race wasn't the problem, increasing the altitude was. The extra 17.7 km detour the ultra-marathoners had to endure was easily one of the most heartbreaking things you'd ever want to witness in a race. I remember it quite distinctly. While the 42 km runners continued on the gradual path, we had to continue higher, over several mountain ridges. For hours on end, we climbed higher and higher, and we were running slower than before.

It probably didn't help that my GPS watch was not accurate whatsoever; but to my best calculations, we had completed 59 km, which was a tad off by 25.5 km. Mentally, this threw my thinking off. I thought we were only a few miles away when there was still such a long distance to go. I already had many post-race antics planned out, only to realize I was still a long way from the finish.

It was mentioned at the race briefing the night prior that if it got too dark to continue, we were allowed to spend the night at a nearby lodge and continue the race the next morning, but we'd get a three-hour penalty.

Fast-forward to 5:30 p.m. I had finally reached the small village of Nah La with my climbing friend Craig. It made sense that we finish the race together, however, neither of us had eaten anything more than a couple muesli bars. We were very close to making the choice of staying at a lodge for the night. We needed the rest, but we didn't want to be penalized with a three-hour penalty. We got some soup from the warm tea house. I thought, "How badass would it be if we continued the race throughout the night?"

Bravely and with determination, we decided there was no point in staying in now. We would just finish the race even, if we got in after midnight! The next six hours sucked out more mental strength from us, compounded by the stress of the two weeks leading up to the trip. The unsurfaced terrain and continuous rises and drops in altitude totally messed with our heads, as if they weren't messed up enough already.

However, crossing that finish line was one surreal feeling to experience. What seemed like a race to some was merely a day of surviving high altitude and the most rugged terrain I've ever dealt with.

In essence, momentum is the driver that keeps us held back from complacency. From someone who has managed to transform his life from things seeming impossible to get out of a rabbit hole, to the pride I felt after completing all my races, is nothing short of a miracle. I am out of that lead mine now and have been shot up into the stratosphere. It's all due to being hungry to get the greatness out of me by pushing the limits and helping others along the way.

HERE'S TO SOCIAL IMPACT!

Similar to my story of creating something from nothing purely from emotion, it brings me to a flashback in my journey. It's a story of what you wouldn't believe was possible but is known for greatness. You may have noticed at the front of the book there was a joint testimonial from a couple of lads, Daniel Flynn and Jarryd Burns. They are two of the three cofounders from the emerging social enterprise, Thankyou, which was formerly known as Thankyou Water.

Toward the start of 2017, I was introduced to Daniel Flynn's book, *Chapter One*, and I was instantly blown. I couldn't put the book down! It was such a captivating story it had me all ears, how three kids wanted to change the world simply by eradicating global poverty in one of the most creative ways possible.

It all started with Dan noticing a statistic of how over a

billion people in the world were living in extreme poverty—less than $1.25 a day. It's insane how easily we can access resources these days. It's like a privilege to have clean water, shelter, and good food in developing countries around the world.

Dan came across another statistic: how the bottled water industry is currently valued at $100 billion per year. It's a ludicrous number that could easily be the amount to solve the global poverty crisis. So, over the past decade, Dan has built a social enterprise (not a charity) as the managing director with his best friend, Jarryd Burns (CFO), and his wife, Justine (CMO), that focuses on one of the biggest problems in the world.

I highly recommend the *Chapter One* book as their story is full of hardships and momentum. There are plenty of times when you think they are about to crumble and then they somehow miraculously solve the situations through sheer creativity. They've managed to tackle feats that other brands would foresee as impossible, but they never let that get to them. That's resilience at its finest, which always gets my attention.

Being absolutely mesmerized with their story, I knew I had to collaborate with Thankyou in the near future. I sensed there was something about the rise and fall of building a brand that really resonated with The Wounded

Pelicans, of which I'm one half. I had decided then and there that I would figure out how to persuade Thankyou to collaborate with me. I knew it might be a mission in itself, since I had no direct connections and didn't know anyone who knew their team. It took me two months just to get their attention, but the persistence paid off.

Chapter One is built on persistence and I knew they'd give me a chance to speak to them, even if I had to call and email their employees every day. I felt I could get in touch with someone who would listen to me. Then, all of a sudden, I had their attention. "Your idea sounds great, Tofe. How would you like to collaborate with Thankyou?" Well, I had an idea in mind, but it had to be bold enough to blend with their efforts and align with both our visions.

That's when I came up with a 100 km Water Walk, where each participant would carry fifty-five pounds of water on their shoulders for 100 km. Notice I said *on their shoulders*, not in a backpack where the weight is distributed on the hips. Why on earth would anyone want to do that? They'd enter the race to represent those around the world who carry water from village to village over marathon-plus distances. Not to mention, the water isn't clean half the time!

Antony and I were accustomed to tackle these absurd and extreme endurance events, so I thought we would replicate the struggles of poverty-stricken youth. We'd do it over a ridiculous distance during the coldest time of the year, finishing at the Thankyou headquarters in Collingwood, VIC. Nothing like this had been done for Thankyou, so this is where we could make it happen.

Bold ideas and social impact were the alignment, and what we could raise would go to a copy of *Chapter One*, their book that funds the Thankyou brand. Some of you will recognize that, like *Chapter One*, this book is also a pay-what-you-think concept. I was so fascinated by the idea that when I was with Dan at the Thankyou headquarters after the Water Walk, I personally asked him if it would be okay if I used it for my own book. He replied, "Of course, man! I didn't even come up with the 'pay-what-you-think' idea. It's been used in restaurants here in Melbourne and other things, so go for it!"

The 100 km Water Walk was a one-of-a-kind event, an adventure in itself with all its failures. The things that didn't go to plan during the twenty-six-hour escapade included things like problems with the water apparatus we had to carry. They were attached only fifteen minutes before start time, and the only way we had the jerry cans attached to the bamboo post were through zip-ties, which seemed to keep snapping off every twenty minutes. Luckily, our support crew went on a mission in the morning shopping for backup zip-ties.

Then at the first 22 km mark, we went from pavement

and civilization to grassy highway next to cars flying at highway speed. By the time we reached the halfway mark, every bit of weight had magnified to the extent that it felt like a mix of nerve damage and constant pounding on our feet. I began thinking I'd rather be anywhere else but here right at this moment. But it just added to the challenge. The first 50 km is always the easiest, or so they say!

Everything from having to change up the circuit because security wouldn't let us through, to monstrous blood blisters, to below-zero temperatures at 3:00 a.m. in Werribee, were only some of the hiccups we encountered. But you learn to adapt in spite of these setbacks on a project like this. All we cared about was getting to the Thankyou headquarters by 10:00 a.m. the following day. We didn't care if it was hailing or snowing. We were on a mission.

Arriving at the finish point at the Thankyou headquarters in Collingwood, VIC, had us feeling full of joy. It was the dopamine rush we needed to fuel that last thrust of energy up those office stairs. Team members from Thankyou, as well as our main support guy, Travis Ireland, were there helping us push through those last few kilometers. It's hard to explain that feeling of emotion after an event like that, but I can tell you, it's one that will stick in my memory for a very long time—especially when I have the chance to tell the tale to my grandkids.

Along with finishing at the Thankyou headquarters, it was an absolute pleasure to work with Dan, Jarryd, and their amazing crew. What they've achieved over this past decade is astonishing, and to be welcomed with open hearts was the icing on the cake. We were genuinely treated like family, and we indulged in the true experience of what Thankyou is about.

FINAL TAKE ON MOMENTUM

As you could probably tell with the culmination of how momentum is important, it's what keeps things alive. Where motivation is only effective to light the fire, momentum and discipline are what keeps fanning the flame.

"It's vital to spend each day trying to be a little wiser than you were when you woke up. Discharge your duties faithfully and well. Step by step you get

ahead, but not necessarily in fast spurts. But you build discipline by preparing for fast spurts. Slug it out one inch at a time, day by day. At the end of the day, if you live long enough, most people get what they deserve."

—CHARLIE MUNGER

CHAPTER 7

REWIRING AUTOMATIC NEURAL PATHWAYS

MAKING FEAR YOUR BEST FRIEND

"Left foot, right foot; keep on moving. That's the mantra my brain is playing over and over to get me through the remaining sixteen hours on my noble steed with a monotonous conveyor belt underneath my blistered feet. This treadmill was a gentle stallion at first, but the sun is piercing through the marquee at such a rapid rate, the only encapsulating area of shade my body can attest to is the platform I'm running on. If anything, the likelihood of jumping off has increased substantially as I turn the notch from eight to eleven, and my urge to stop and set the bloody thing on fire seems like the better option. While I would never commit arson, suddenly a handful of strangers enter the realm of the sweaty and noisy constant movement that ironically is going in no direction. Their enlightened presence enters with plenty of warmth, enough to enjoy what I'm assimilating. With a friendly hello came esoteric tears of joy and an ocean of gratification. An abstruse connection between the three feet of these folk and my fatigued body gave the rush I needed to continue on those final sixteen hours. Taking on such a challenge showed what the human species is capable of and it expresses itself in such a selfless way. The funds would be given to those who battle overbearing, gargantuan wars of cancer, so a measly twenty-four hours on a treadmill isn't even worthy of comparison. The tears from those I've never met had merely started to rewire the way I thought about life. It had a profound effect on them and myself that there was hope. Certainly it was purely a good deed created out of the struggles from years ago. Who would've thought adversity would be a good thing?" —September 3, 2016

Reading this chapter heading may sound quite technical, but to simplify what your neural pathways are, it's your nervous system; the network of nerve cells and fibers that transmit nerve impulses between parts of the body. Essentially, as we're on this path of discovery transforming worthless habits and superseding them with new purposeful ones, it's inevitable how your automatic neural pathways will be rewired to suit the situation.

In this chapter, this is when the methods start to become unconventional, and this will help maintain your focus. Why would unconventionalism be practiced? Because it's appealing to the eye as the regular pattern is broken. Simply, our brains are wired for novelty.

Unlike the previous chapters, this one will contain a different vernacular, a language used to really explain as we go deep within the psychological and scientific reasoning of how to be greater human beings. One way is to understand why our brain reacts to certain scenarios known as the "Oh shit!" moments.

"OH, SHIT" MOMENTS

Many memorable experiences I've had were during times when the amygdala in my brain was red hot and fear was trying to take over. Some of you will be reading this wondering what the hell an amygdala is. Well, as per the image below, it's the fear center of the brain located in the emotional section known as our limbic system.

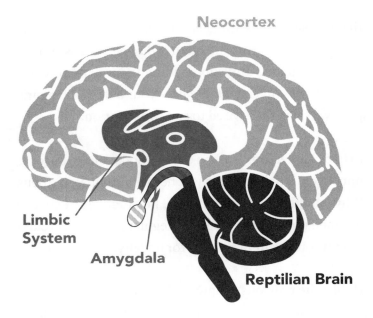

Neocortex

Limbic System

Amygdala

Reptilian Brain

This straightforward diagram of the brain is labelled as three separate sections, each of which I've translated into simpler terminology.

- **REPTILIAN BRAIN**. Its incredible survivability is out to protect us; it's the logic we still carry from our ten-thousand-plus-year-old ancestors. It's known as Survival Brain, Ancestral Brain, Crocodile Brain, and Primal Brain.
- **LIMBIC SYSTEM**. This is the instinct that drives our emotional language and emotional intelligence; it controls our basic emotions (fear, pleasure, anger) and actuates hunger, sex, dominance, and care of offspring. It also contains the hippocampus, our memory center.

- **NEOCORTEX**. This is used for decision making and is our logicality. It's where our higher cortical regions control thinking, planning, dreaming, imagining, and long-term consequential thinking happens.
- **AMYGDALA**. The fear center is located in the limbic system, where we produce fight-or-flight responses.

As we grow older, we become more risk-averse. There's a reason why teens are more likely to take on something that looks fun and take more risks—because their higher cortical regions haven't fully matured yet. That will happen at the age of twenty-one to twenty-three for females and twenty-three to twenty-six for males. Until then, those projections that help us think consequently are not necessarily in place, which is why people are far more prone to take risks during those years.

Regarding suicide, it's one of the reasons why teen boys, when they're depressed, are more likely to carry through with it. Their brains are not fully functioning and are not fully connected. It's part of the reason why they behave in such a way, because they're not completely aware of the risks associated with what's happening. Understanding that part of the brain helps us understand that the center part of the brain, the limbic system, has the amygdala as well as the hippocampus. Our hippocampus is our memory center. When we're first born, our explicit memories occur when the "feeling" memory is laid down into a long-term memory system that comes onboard around two years of age.

But we have both implicit and explicit memories. Implicit memories are when experiences haven't transformed into long-term memory and haven't been hit by the hippocampus. There may be a sense of remembering a grandparent's house or a childhood school and then you go to a place, but it isn't a factual reconstruction memory of the place, yet you do have a sense of feeling an emotion from being there.

> "Implicit memory when it's encoded and just stays in that pure form goes into storage where it just changes in my synaptic connections. It's purely a set of raw unconscious body memory packets."
>
> —DANIEL SIEGEL

So, when we're in a place of danger—think of the twin towers tragedy from 9/11 as an example—and when people saw it on TV or experienced what was happening in person, their implicit and explicit memory system was heavily in play. They're amygdala was firing and they were freaking out because their fight-or-flight response took control. Some were very traumatized. That's what happens when we're in a place and we can't make sense of what's going on; there is so much cortisol, it's through the roof. There's too much of the stress hormone in our brains and we're so heavily focused on survival that the experience is not transversed into an explicit memory. It's not laying down into a long-term memory system.

Therefore, people don't necessarily have a narrative of trauma that they've experienced, yet they can make contact with the feeling, so they might not have a memory. That explains why we can have lapses in our memory of traumatic events like emotional triggers. It's extremely traumatic when the brain actually shuts down to make a strong narrative around what happened. A person quite close to someone who may have died will cancel that memory of what it feels or looks like. That's because the brain is so focused on survival mode that their memory is not translated into a long-term, embedded memory. However, they do have a sense about what's going on in that moment.

Going back to why we focus on the negative things in life, our brains are wired so that if survival mechanism—the evolutionary function of our brains—finds something to be a threat to us, we react in a way that may seem perilous to others. But we're just subconsciously doing what we think is the best for us. Essentially, we're priming ourselves to really focus in on danger and then we try to develop behavioral strategies to avoid that situation if it happens again.

When I delivered my first keynote to a large audience, I got plenty of great feedback as well as constructive criticism. I remember the latter more than the compliments, if anything. However, after working on where I lacked, that criticism has shifted to the positive side of things when I'm delivering a speech today.

Now, if the experience is too traumatic, sometimes our brains will bypass that explicit memory system and we don't lay down a factual memory of what actually happened. We remember the feeling of what that horrible email felt like, and we remember the words that were in that email because the implicit memory system lays down in a more physical way. So, it has an emotion associated with it. It might not have a story with what that email said, but we have the feelings, which can be triggered the next time we give a speech and someone gives us criticism. It can trigger that implicit memory system if it's been traumatic enough.

Our Limbic System has a number of parts that create this complex structure of emotional components. It works very strongly and is well-integrated with the incredibly primitive brain stem. The emotional memory system is primed to avoid any peril and is responsible for activating a fear alarm.

The higher cortical regions are the newest and most evolved parts of the brain. When we are really activating in a fear state, the projections (neural pathways) between our limbic system and higher cortical areas are disconnected. To give you an example of that, you might have seen a toddler throwing a tantrum, having a meltdown you could say. Well, what's happening for that child is he is totally immobilized by his limbic system and the projections to his higher cortical regions are not working. So, if Mum says, "Stop crying, Jimmy, I'll get you a chocolate," or, "You wait till we get home and I'll tell your father what you've done!" all of her reasoning is not going to help that toddler who's in the emotionally activated state. He's just been totally hijacked by his limbic (emotional) system. The projections toward the cortex that help him say, "Well, perhaps I should calm down now because I need to think about the consequences" are not going to happen.

The same process happens for us as adults. We have meltdowns of our own when our limbic system hijacks our decision-making process and consequential thinking. It takes over the ability to care for ourselves and it creates a story of what's happening. "Okay, I'm feeling really upset right now, and I need to take time out and get a breath of fresh air." We see this sometimes happening during a conflict. It's a fight that might occur when people are drinking. They're not really able to make connections to those consequential pathways.

MAKE FEAR YOUR BEST FRIEND

How do you make yourself less prone to fight-or-flight and trauma? By making fear your best friend.

Trying anything for the first time will have us wondering, "What on earth am I doing? It's probably a good idea if I head home and watch Netflix instead." Initially, when you have a first experience with fear, regardless of whether it's extreme or not, you will be able to increase those projections between your limbic system and higher cortical areas. For me, I've trained myself by taking on absurd and extreme endurance challenges that have allowed me to get my brain accustomed to fear. By doing that, I reduce the activation of the fight-or-flight response.

FEAR VS. TRUST

Essentially, a tough situation will result into two scenarios: fear or trust. They can't function together at the same time.

You either experience trust or you experience fear. There's a point when you need to take a leap of faith. Completing a set of ladder crossings over open crevasses in the Everest region rewired my emotional thinking. My past experiences of mastery from other events helped me to down-regulate the activation of the amygdala, either by holding my breath or by using a narrative. In that instant, I would create a story that I either consciously or unconsciously bring to mind that tells my brain, "I've done tough things and I've got this, bro!" That narrative helps to calm down the activity of the amygdala. It's as if my experiences and memories with pushing my mind and body to new heights are the validation my brain needs to take those crucial leaps of faith.

In my personal life, I work hard on building resilience, which has enabled me to stop that process, similar to what occurred for that toddler who had the meltdown. I was unable to connect with those higher processes. Through repetition and mastery, I'm able to move quickly past stressful moments, and relay them back to the Practical Resilience formula. This is the discipline (repetition) and obsession (mastery) I'm experiencing in the mindset pillar.

Throughout this journey of making ourselves the best versions we can be, it never occurs in a linear motion but it's more of an adventure. Pushing through the stressful climbs increases cortisol, and when we reach the top of the mountain, we know that it was all worth it. There's more dopamine than anything seeing those beautiful sights.

DOPAMINE VS. CORTISOL

Dopamine, known as the happy hormone, is primarily associated with our reward system. It plays a really important role in behavior rehearsal, whether we drink coffee and feel good, resulting in us ordering another one, or we go for a run and feel good afterward. It increases our chance of doing it again because we feel good. Cortisol, on the other hand, is a stress hormone. It can build up over time, and wears down people's immune functions and resilience. It can have serious psychological effects. In essence, we want to experience more dopamine. Ironically, putting ourselves through purposeful suffering will increase our dopamine.

APPLYING EMOTIONAL INTELLIGENCE TO EVERYDAY LIVING

I briefly touched on emotional intelligence earlier in this book, but what is it exactly? Emotional Intelligence (EI) is the capacity to control and express one's emotions, and to handle interpersonal relationships judiciously and empathetically.

In the following everyday scenarios, you'll discover things

that have happened to me in the past and how I was able to push through them. Before relaying these stories to you, I want to mention again that adversity is a blessing in disguise, because it's your greatest teacher in life. With each sticky situation, I'll explain how I was able to recognize what was going on through EI and what I've learned from each experience.

1. HAVING A BUSINESS VENTURE GO HAYWIRE

EI: The specific path I was taking was probably not aligned with my purpose, hence the bad decisions, one after the other.

SOLUTION: I realized that almost every business will go through ups and downs, but it's more important to have the reason why. When our values are established right from the start, we can build the foundation to prevent the pathway leading us into turmoil. Any business ventures from this point had this mentality to ensure any past mistakes wouldn't happen again.

2. HAVING MY HEART BROKEN BY A GIRL

EI: Knowing that I have to be the person I'd date when I look at it from their perspective.

SOLUTION: Focus on staying kind, caring, and really

being there during the hardships to increase the chances of a stronger and long-lasting relationship.

3. ENDURED AN INJURY DURING A RUNNING RACE

EI: My body was warning me that I might be putting too much stress and strain on that specific area.

SOLUTION: I've learned how to condition and rapidly increase the strength of my body by going through strength training and conditioning. To go from wearing strapping tape for every event in 2016 because of a recurring niggle, to not having to worry about it, has prevented me from becoming injury-prone. Not only is this a physical relief, but it's mentally emancipating.

4. GOT REJECTED BY AN EMAIL INQUIRY

EI: Like other brands, they're just super busy, and just because they said no doesn't mean they won't change their mind later on.

SOLUTION: I'm not the only one who has ever been rejected by the same company. When they reject me through email, I'll just approach them through their other social media channels. Or maybe I've pitched to them incorrectly. At least this feedback teaches me to experiment with other ways of contacting someone, and I can split-test my approach to see what works best.

5. I STRUGGLED WITH HIGH ALTITUDE DURING A SUMMIT CLIMB ABOVE 6,100 METERS

EI: My brain was experiencing less oxygen and I actually felt drunk. I would instantly feel better if I descended to a lower altitude where I could breathe a little easier. Then I could head back up to try again the following day.

SOLUTION: Don't rush when it comes to altitude; the nasty bitch can kill you.

Remember that the key to getting out of the "Oh, shit!" moments is to adapt! With each solution, I'd decided that I had to be nimble and think quickly on the fly. Over-thinking causes decision paralysis. That's when "good enough is perfect" comes into play. Time is our most valuable asset, so don't ponder those things that can be solved in a fraction of what you thought. Life is a game of speed chess. We can't see the future, but it's a smart tool to have along when you need a solution before things start to fall apart.

Take the injury dilemma above; this is a common debacle in sports and everyday living. How we approach the physical setback can show true resilience. I could've stopped running when the physio said I should stop or when my knee gave out during several races. I managed to stay persistent and took up strength training to eliminate the pain and to pursue my purpose.

Maybe you haven't experienced any type of endurance-related sport that can drive your future movements during stressful periods, but you're not entirely empty-handed. You use artillery and ammunition to propel yourself. I'm talking about any adversity you've come across in life beforehand, such as a breakup, death in the family, loss of a job, betrayal of a close one, etc.

It all comes back to perspective. You know there's a moment from your past that you think was the scariest time, but you got through it. Now, as you're facing another challenge, you know that this time is not nearly as bad. You can reflect on the past, but you have to be careful not to delve too deep and think about the mistakes you've made. Since you've already been through hell before, your next challenge will be a walk in the park.

Before you know it, you'll skip the process of fear, and you will trust what's going on instead. With plenty of repetition and discipline in building this style of mental resilience, your confidence and mastery will grow to a level that allows you to handle any challenge. You've taken that leap of faith because you have the tools to calm your emotional arousal.

One of my idols, Joe De Sena (Spartan Race Founder) speaks of a concept known as "purposeful suffering." It's a method that shifts your frame of reference into believing what's actually tough. I was fortunate enough to speak with Joe one on one, and I got his take on purposeful suffering.

TOFE: Joe, you've spoken on the topic of purposeful suffering where you'll deliberately put yourself through tough situations to increase resilience. This is something I've taken on since I first heard about you in 2015, especially with ultramarathons. I've signed up for the longest distance races every time. I've noticed it's a great way to increase mental strength and give me a thicker skin. What are some practical tips anyone can apply when getting started today with purposeful suffering, especially if they want to increase their resilience?

JOE DE SENA: The fastest way to build grit and resistance is to experience it. I suggest taking up the following:

- Burpees
- Cold showers
- Training outside in bad weather
- Fasting

Joe's argument explains how putting our bodies through deliberate stress will actually make us happier in the long haul. Why is that?

When the mind and body are experiencing any sort of stress (working out, adversity, etc.), we start digging deep, hoping to come to a solution. When we do, we have a sense of victory that makes it all worth it. The dopamine in our brain (happiness hormone) is red hot, and we want to tell the world about it.

DO MATERIAL ITEMS LIKE A NEW CAR OR HOUSE GIVE US A SAFER AND EASIER WAY TO BE HAPPY?

Yes, there is some happiness to an extent, but we become susceptible to habituation. You may have a little Volkswagen Polo and see a nice sedan and you think it's enough impetus to purchase one. After a few weeks, you're over it, and then we come across that Range Rover. Rinse and repeat until the Rolls Royce is the next goal. But you'll be constantly chasing this tail and you'll be far from happy if this is your primary goal in life.

Owning ravishing items is nice and all, but there's no grit required in obtaining them. Yes, you may have worked your arse off this past year to save up for that new house, but if it's happiness you're after, then you are better off taking on something fearful and sticking with it. It will align with your intrinsic motivation and, more importantly, you will attain a greater sense of self-compassion. Whereas, the extrinsic goals, like getting a new car, that we think will make us happy are not reconnecting with our value system.

Practicing purposeful suffering within our relationships in either business, romance, or friendships is always successful, and those relationships are longer-lasting if they've been through the stress together. It comes down to passionate vs. companionate relationships, a study researched in the book *The Happiness Hypothesis* by NYU Professor, Jonathan Haidt.

1. PASSIONATE RELATIONSHIPS are great at the start, but they die off too early. It's because one or both partners is moving too quickly, and when stress arises from both sides, then one or both are over each other.
2. Whereas COMPANIONATE RELATIONSHIPS stay strong over time and get better as each year continues. These relationships have been through the hardships together and continue to do so during any setbacks.

THE TIME COURSE OF THE TWO KINDS OF LOVE
(SHORT VS LONG RUN)

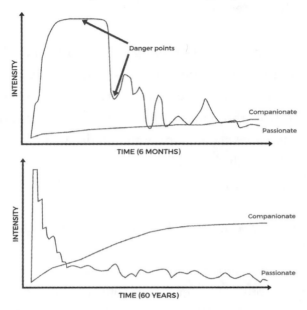

From *The Happiness Hypothesis: Finding Modern Truth in Ancient Wisdom* by Jonathan Haidt copyright © 2005. Reprinted by permission of Basic Books, an imprint of Perseus Books, LLC, a subsidiary of Hachette Book Group, Inc.

PRIMING YOUR BRAIN TO SAY YES

By saying yes to every challenge, you quickly become fearless and bulletproof.

As mentioned earlier, we confront a tough situation by being in either a fearful or trusting mindset. Too many people are living in **FEAR** instead of living in **TRUST**. As for me, I know what it's like to be living in both situations. Right now, I'm in that constant state of fearlessness, which is why I can take up such extreme endurance events or tasks on a whim without freaking out. Literally, I feel invincible. It's a wonderful feeling. I don't do it to the point where I think I can take on a moving car and survive the impact; that's stupidity.

It gets to a point where I reflect on the past and ask myself if what I've dealt with before is harder than this task or challenge (of course it was harder to deal with depression and anxiety). This paradigm shift instantly gives me a level-headed attitude, and it enables me to push through to the finish line. This comes back into perspective when you start skipping a step in the process. This isn't meant to make you freak out. Instead, you should feel in touch with the fear step and your current narrative. You should be saying to yourself and in your mind, "I got this, bro!"

HOW DEMOCRACY KILLS OUR LIMITS AND THINKING

Limitations are everywhere and who we choose to listen to becomes the deciding factor of what we put our minds to. People are not out to help us when they say, "That won't work," but who said it won't work for us just because it didn't work for them?

Take the marathon as an example. Nike is working on breaking the two-hour marathon record, a timeframe that would've seemed impossible decades ago. Yes, there are always skeptics, yet with the progress since it's been a priority has been substantial. They'll soon be saying, "To smash out a sub-two marathon, do this." Well, I won't be doing it anytime soon. I'm still working on sub three-hour time.

Isn't it funny that when negative emotions arrive, they're magnified to the extreme? It's probably a good correlation on why bad news sells, because we only take real notice about anything bad when we're on the resisting side. Why is that, by the way? Well, it's how we humans are hard-wired. Some people can take negativity better than others. It's the same on social media. When you receive a bad comment over a good one, you resist the truth. And even when you receive an insult as opposed to a compliment, you have the choice of responding and regretting it later, or ignoring the post. However, it's most likely that you'll always remember the negative remarks.

Why does this occur? You could easily say that any negative emotion is tied to the trauma of a bad past memory or some sort of fear. Early in this chapter, I explained that the brain contains an actual fear center known as the amygdala. It's what controls our fight-or-flight response and any rationale in that regard. If in any moment we're startled, then it's Code Red! It can trigger any amount of irrational thinking.

> **"First, people are generally rational, and their thinking is normally sound. Second, emotions such as fear, affection, and hatred explain most of the occasions on which people depart from rationality."**
>
> **—DANIEL KAHNEMANN**

For myself, I'd be taking hits from certain jokes that end up compounding over time, which would result in an imploding mess. But instead of reacting to a negative comment or insult, I have to remind myself that my actions could have even more negative results, so I just walk in the other direction.

Being an emotional person can be tough at times, but it's

also your greatest strength. I'm not talking about emotional as if you're crying and throwing tantrums. I'm talking about being passionate. Almost every decision has some level of illogicality that makes you respond from a gut reaction. You feel this in relationships when you are ready to date a person.

In my past, I'd take everything literally to heart. I'm not just talking about insults; big decisions would almost take me down the illogical route.

Following are several examples from my past. Maybe you've gone through these too:

1. Taking up a business idea with a person overseas whom I'd never met and putting in $12,000 of my own money without evaluating the business. My first angel investment gone wrong!
2. Falling in love in a country I couldn't live in.
3. Working in a job for much longer than I should have.

EVERYONE MAKES MISTAKES

Yes, everyone makes mistakes, but here's the catch...they don't have to be your mistakes! One thought to reduce stress and cortisol levels.

You know that feeling when you're driving to work and

you can't remember getting there? You've arrived at your usual carpark and don't even remember the six sets of traffic lights and three roundabouts you saw along the way. That is autonomy, my friend!

Your brain is so used to travelling down that same route, you could do it with your eyes closed. It's as if there's a large field of high grass and a row of grass is mown so deep, you can see the pathway quite clearly. Now, that field of high grass is your brain, metaphorically speaking. We all have habits and our favorite ways of doing things. Our field of high grass has several mown rows of grass, but here's the catch: a field can only hold so much.

The way to reduce autonomy is through present-focus living, that is, living in the now. It correlates to meditations because the point is to gain our self-awareness and keep our emotional intelligence at an all-time high. The last thing you want to do is get to the end of your day and have no conception of what you did. So, this is where we are constantly experimenting to keep our brains away from functioning on autopilot. We must live in the moment.

TOOLS FOR PRESENT-FOCUS LIVING

In this section, I'm going to show you practical tools you can use to ensure you're living in a present-focus living environment. Here are a few tips to help with everyday routine:

- Change up your drive to work and anywhere else you normally travel to on a regular basis (gym, meetings, social gatherings).
- Take up new activities that will thought-provoke your mind. Try that capoeira class or a month of Bikram yoga.
- Try going a month without watching TV to keep your mind away from constant adverts and negative news headlines.
- Sign up for a half-marathon if the couch is your best friend.
- Attend a live music gig if you're constantly confined to the house.

The majority of the world lives in fear and autonomy mode. You now have an opportunity to change that by living a life of having **TRUST** in a fluid motion and where **FEAR** is your best friend. You will rewire your neural pathways to become proactive instead of reactive in fearful situations. It will look appealing to others because you can handle your shit when it hits the fan.

We can't remember everything, which is why you have to keep learning and replace those bad habits with new ones. It'll be a rusty process at the start. Like anything new, you want to hone those habits until they become natural, where it doesn't feel like work. When you brush your teeth each day and night, you don't set a reminder to do it. You just know to do it before going to bed. When you wake up, you just brush your teeth without prompting. Because you've done it every day, it's a habit, and you know it's good for good dental hygiene. The same thing goes for lyrics. You might hear a catchy song you adore and listen to it over and over and sing it until you know it by heart. Then when the song comes on the radio, you can belt out every word without any trouble.

REPLACING THOSE BAD HABITS WITH GREAT ONES!

You might recognize and already implement the following bad habits in your daily schedule without realizing it. Lucky for you, I have a solution to bring you immense change for the future. Look at how to replace bad habits with great ones in the table that follows.

BAD HABITS (CURRENT)	GREAT HABITS (REPLACING WITH)
No exercise	Get more movement—take up a sport or fitness routine of some sort (running/walking/surfing/swimming/etc.)
Constantly scrolling on Facebook and social media for the sake of it	Read more books or listen to podcasts and audiobooks
Living in fear	Do something scary every day to reduce fear
Too risk-averse, living in the comfort zone	Be experimental to stay in the present moment
Consuming all information from the news that focuses on every negative media piece	Literally stop watching the news and instantly notice how positive your perception on life becomes

The key to habit-building is to start small or you'll riddle yourself with overwhelm. Once you're in a rhythm, there's a great chance you'll maintain consistency and meet other like-minded folks.

YOUR VIBE ATTRACTS YOUR TRIBE

Known to many as the law of attraction, the brain will filter out any irrelevancy. That brand new car you bought? You'll see it everywhere you go. When you become a parent for the first time, you'll be attracted to other parents.

Donald O. Hebb, a renowned Canadian neuropsychologist, discovered this back in the 1940s from an experiment with nanoparticles when neurons could have the ability to cluster together, creating a unified response. Furthermore, "Neurons that fire together, wire together."

Or, if we want to get real specific, this Hebbian Law elaborated that when an axon of cell A is near enough to excite cell B, and repeatedly or persistently takes part in firing it, some growth process or metabolic change takes place in one or both cells, such that A's efficiency, as one of the cells firing B, is increased.

I got a real glimpse of this concept during my rehabilitation process when I started running as an escapism to get my health (mentally and physically) back on track. At first it was a lonely feeling, but before I knew it, I'd met other runners. Maybe they weren't running for the same reasons, but I was meeting other like-minded people. This was my first true taste of immersion. It was such a pure feeling. Instantly, my constant worrying simmered considerably so I could think and sleep better. It does help when you exercise with endorphins pumping.

The more events I took part in during 2015, the more my mind opened to what I was capable of doing. I was loving every moment of that new challenge. By the time it was 2016, endurance was a main priority in my life. As the years went on, members of the running community would notice The Wounded Pelicans at each event.

Surprise in seeing us at each race had sparked curiosity and we wondered why people kept noticing us. We explained what our project and yearly goals were about, and almost everyone's immediate responses were expressions of feeling stoked. Eventually, however, we were asked, "Hey, there's this event coming up next week. Are you boys keen to compete in it?"

After a few seconds, our general response would be, "Fuck it, let's do it!"

One thing led to another and we undoubtedly said yes every time—whether it was a very arduous and steep half-marathon or a 160 km ultramarathon in the forest—developing this, "She'll be right!" attitude (a common Australian saying also translated as "It's all good, bro!"). It's not like we're elite athletes or anything special, yet soon we heard people referring to us as "those crazy kids."

The plan wasn't to become figures in the sport, it was to push ourselves. But when you experience selfless gratitude to raise funds and awareness for those who really need it, you want to do more. Needless to say, the initial thirteen events soon became twenty-five, then thirty-three, and then finally, a whopping forty! Literally, forty events in one year. Yes, there are others who have done sixty or even one hundred events in one year, but to transition from thirteen to forty is three times more than we expected.

To put that into perspective, we sacrificed every damn weekend and an endless amount of time and energy, and it was worth every fucking second. We were welcomed into the running and endurance community, which had become our second family.

There are millions of people like yourself who want what's best for them and to transform their lives for the future. Like my reason to be a runner surely was based on my desire to be joining forces with those who use the sport for escapism. Ironically, we are running from our demons to propel us to the end. A twenty-six-mile marathon may sound like a long time to be on your feet, but trust me, the adversity you've been through in life was way worse.

OVERCOMING THE DARK TIMES

If you've ever experienced the loss of job, a parent's divorce, your own divorce, or a drug relapse, then you know these were very dark times. So, why not use those tough times to drive you through those mental and physical walls? I'd like you to realize that your past may have been a very scary and traumatic time, but if you can push through that situation, then completing a marathon is nothing in retrospect.

A training run might take an hour, but it'll be over before I know it. The pain in my past was a much worse experience to endure. Then as the next event arises, I can use the mental strength strategy from previous races (whether it was long in distance or not) because the same thing applies. During every event, I will encounter a sense of difficulty, but all I have to do is just use each strategy in my mindset to believe that it's a training run for the next one.

Unintentionally, I've acquired this "no-excuses attitude" to face fear straight on, but in a way, I'm not abashed from the process. If anything, it kind of gets me excited. Yes, every journey starts from somewhere; mine was rock-bottom, though I don't let it get to me so I could get on with what I needed to do to keep striving. I'm talking about a relentless mindset.

Tim Grover talks about this in his book *Relentless*. From his experience coaching Michael Jordan, Kobe Bryant, Dwyane Wade, and many other prolific NBA players, Grover explicitly explains that the distinguishing factor between a hall-of-fame player and a great player is their mindset and discipline. There's a reason why MJ is the GOAT—because he's legendary.

Tim speaks of his philosophy of the coolers, cleaners, and the closers. That is, good, great, and legendary. To be in the closer category, not only are you incredibly proactive in your field, but you've set the bar so high for yourself, you're kilometers ahead of whoever is in second place. I know I've got a ways to go before I get there, but I can definitely envision it happening.

NOT PART OF A COMMUNITY? JOIN ONE!

"What if I don't like running, Tofe? What other communities can I be part of?" Hey, I'm not pushing you to be a runner. I do recommend taking up a sport or a type of fitness routine, because you're integrating both health and well-being at once. That's integration #lifehack. Communities are everywhere. Small businesses meet up every week, and even the infamous Sexpo (sex expedition) is an unbelievable community, in the most erotic way possible.

Churches, sports, religion, and free masonry are also types of community groups. In essence, a community is a family-orientated group of people who practice the same values.

Even if you're part of your local church and attend weekly meetings with business owners, I highly recommend joining a fitness movement. It's scientifically proven that implementing an active lifestyle into your regimen will increase your happiness a hundredfold, at least. And who cares what everyone else thinks when you're immersed with other like-minded people? They've got their own problems to worry about.

What are a few of the current fitness movements in the world today that you can be part of?

- Running community: road/trail/ultra

- Obstacle course racing: Spartan/Tough Mudder/Ninja Warrior
- All-around strength: Cross-fit/gym/boot camps
- Surfing/stand-up paddle boarding
- Ball sports: rugby/tennis/soccer/football/volleyball/ etc.
- Yoga: Bikram (hot)/Vinyasa
- Multidisciplinary sports: triathlon/adventure racing
- Walking

CONNECTING WITH YOUR COMMUNITY

What emotions will you experience when you immerse yourself in a new fitness community? It's quite a roller-coaster of a journey, but it's a fun roller-coaster.

THE EMOTIONAL ROLLERCOASTER OF JOINING A COMMUNITY

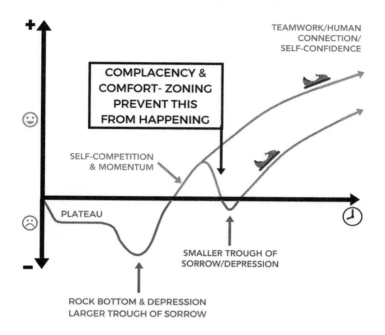

At the end of the day, humans are wired for connection, and that feeling of surrounding yourself with like-minded people helps you become part of your community. You will not only establish new friendships, but it's a priceless feeling being part of a team with those who are on the same journey. Becoming part of a community can benefit everyone.

CHAPTER 8

———

MIND HACKS

SMASHING THROUGH THE MENTAL WALLS

"Thought in, thought out. Constant back-and-forth, constant rinse and repeat. However, now it's 'good thought in' and 'disastrous thought out.' Holy shit, I figured out how to hack the mind! I spent years and years trying to figure out how to silence the demons in my head, when really I'll be spending my entire life on that mission; decades of wasted energy. Instead, it's as if I've attained a belt containing all the tools to harness those thoughts. This new mindset will help me finish all my endurance feats I didn't think a human being could possibly complete. What a fucking relief." —November 4, 2016

We always want the simple way out of a task because time is our most valuable commodity. You may think money is more valuable, but when you can lose $30,000, you can regain $30,000 over time. However, you can't reverse time and be five years or even a day younger. So really, today is the youngest day you'll ever be.

I've seen too many people in the world wanting that get-rich-quick-scheme to make money faster, or some fat-blaster ab machine from an infomercial, or even a pill to bring happiness and fulfillment. These may catch your attention, tricking you into believing you can obtain that instant gratification, but that is complete horseshit. There's no such thing. However, what is true is knowing you can create your own foundation to build your life on.

Imagine a house under construction. If the foundation is not constructed correctly from the start, the house will crumble no matter how good the tools and resources are. What I'm saying is, "Get the foundation right from the start!"

You may be contemplating all this and saying to yourself, "Tofe, I thought this chapter was about mind hacks?" It is. I'm just outlining the strategy and telling you that the right path is mandatory and a prerequisite. From there, you can focus on disrupting everyday conventional thinking. Where you should want to quicken the process a little, however, is by learning from the greats, like I have. I've come across several ways that will definitely work for you so that you can avoid becoming the bitch of your own brain.

Before I continue with these mind hacks, I'm going to say again that I'm a thought leader on practical resilience, not on hacking the body to get you your ideal body. I want to give you the artillery to hold yourself together when you find yourself up against a traumatic crisis. I'm not the guy who'll get you to that perfect body. In this book, I'm here to get you on the right path to a six-pack mind, and that's so much more important.

These may sound counter-intuitive but you're actually disrupting the system, in the best possible way. I said at the start of the book that you'll have to trust me on my methods, so just give it a try. Hey, what's the worst that can happen?

Once you've learned to control the little guy inside your head in the face of all the doubt, and you can control the moment as if it's almost self-meditating, then you'll experience the state of flow. (This was mentioned in Chapter 2.) To refresh your memory, flow is a term coined by psychologist Mihaly Czikszentmihali, who describes this concept as the state when you are working at optimal experience and maintaining that level.

MIND HACK #1: SIMULATE A TOUGH DECISION WITH "WHAT'S THE WORST THAT CAN HAPPEN?"

Those six words strung into a sentence are among the most profound you can ask yourself when facing a fearful decision. Instantly, it has us grounded so we know there is always something that makes our current situation look like nothing.

An example of mine is when I was training for a 80 km stand-up paddleboard event for youth adversity. I was asked by the board sponsors if I'd like to train with their team in the weeks leading up to the event. This group of paddleboarders encompassed some of Australia's best riders who have won championships and titles around the world. My first thoughts were, "Uhhh, what are they going to think of me?" I wasn't too experienced in the sport, and to an outsider, it would probably look as if I had taken up running for the first time. Then I simulated the situation with, "What's the worst that can happen?" and straightaway, I realized I'd be fine. I didn't have to go to war or get surgery that day, so this event should be fine. Plus, it's only an hour of training. The event was over before I knew it. My initial thoughts of what they'd think had the fight-or-flight response in my amygdala (fear center of the brain) red hot, but I cooled down. I understood that I was taking up training for a 80 km event, a distance that most of the training group would never have thought about and they're training for their own reasons.

Maybe you're ready to make that career change by working on your passion that's been your hobby for quite some time now. Maybe you can see it possibly being that avenue to quitting your full-time job. Well, this is when you turn it into a side hustle, because you have bills to pay but you're unsure if it's worth the time investing in. Next, ask yourself, "What's the worst that can happen?" You may have to sacrifice your weekends for a while to get the ball rolling quicker, and you may be a little more tired, but if this is what you truly want you'll make it happen, regardless of proving anything to those who didn't think you'd do it.

"I'd rather be tired than broke."

—MARK CUBAN

We often reflect on times with the worst-case scenario and with the fear of what is really the worst thing that will happen. The reason your desired outcome doesn't actually turn out the way you planned is because, so many times, you're immobilized by fear—yet your worst fears don't come true. Somehow, we manage to make it through that situation and the next challenge that confronts us. We make it through that point where we're totally exhausted, but at the end of the day, we've got this!

MIND HACK #2: DO AN EXTRA REP FOR EVERY SET

When you've got a task to do, focus on that little bit extra every time. Running a 5 km training run? Run 6 km instead. Pumping ten reps on the bench press? Press eleven. Reading for fifteen minutes each day? Just read for sixteen minutes.

I know you don't want to do that extra rep, but just do it to mess with your head. It's like the set of dominos in

Chapter 7 about movement. The first one will not knock over the last one straightaway, so start with small incremental increases and you'll begin approaching difficult tasks with ease.

I know when I push that little bit extra, I'm so much happier for it. At the time, it's far from great, until you feel that rush of excitement and triumph when you push that little bit extra. Essentially, you're slowly surpassing what you believed were limits, and it's not a traumatizing experience but a gradual progressive modality. The key with this hack is to increase incrementally because your body is building an Evolutionary Stable Strategy (ESS) in the process.

An ESS is a fancier term for negotiating the body and mind with incremental stages in growth to avoid burnout. Have you ever come across a friend who has decided to take up the gym for the first time in years and thinks it'd be a great idea to smash out six sessions a week straightaway? By week two or three, they're over it or they're a little traumatized. It's better to create an ESS and start with one or two sessions a week, building it slowly into your neural pathways so it's easier later on (months away) to train six times a week without burnout or boredom.

So, with every task you have, make it a habit to do a tiny extra. Then, when you come across a tough task, it won't be as difficult as you thought it would be, because you're used to doing extra with everything.

MIND HACK #3: DO SOMETHING SCARY EVERY DAY

Let me define scary. It's anything that gets your heart rate beating faster than usual, and it's fear that may be holding you back. You don't have to bungy jump or swim with sharks (hey, if you feel the need to do this, go for it!). But really, anything new and unfamiliar the first time is going to be fearful.

I practically do this every time I sign up for a new event. Whether it's a 10 km run or the recent 345 km ultramarathon in Scotland I signed up for. I know that any of these events can have me digging so deep mentally that it helps with any adversity. Plus, to be representing Australia for a 61-plus km race is a pretty awesome feeling!

But it comes back down to, "What's the worst that can happen?" I know if I don't sign up for these events, I'll probably be riddled with regret sometime in my future.

Ideally, you want to get the scariest thing done first thing in the morning to make your day easier. Once you've tackled one of the hardest things you could do that day, cognitively, your thinking will change—a paradigm shift. Perspective comes into the realm, creating the thought that, "This isn't so bad." Like I said earlier, something scary can be something small, but what you're creating is a new habit. Yes, it may seem counter-intuitive, but you're rewiring your neural pathways to be able to handle stress.

It's Hebbs Law, baby! "Neurons that fire together, wire together!"

PRACTICAL FEARFUL SITUATION EXAMPLES

Following are examples of some practical fearful situations you could deliberately do today:

- Ice baths
- Cold showers
- Joining a running group for a training session
- Always aim for the biggest event, such as signing up for the marathon instead of the half-marathon. This will increase your mental resilience after pushing more during the event.
- Ask a stranger, "Is there anything I could do to help you today?"

Acting on any of these examples will have you asking, "What's the point of having a cold shower? It's freakin' winter, man." I don't care if it is winter, you're building thicker skin during this process so it'll come naturally to you after enough repetition.

How do you quantify whether you're on the right track with deliberately putting yourself in stressful situations? Until fear is your best friend—you're in the complete trust of what's going on and you're completely cool under pressure, that's how you'll know. A great example of this is that minute just before Usain Bolt takes off for a 100 km sprint. It's incredibly nerve-racking, but he's in complete control of the moment.

"Sign up now, worry about it later."

—RICHARD BRANSON

MIND HACK #4: REGRET FACTORING

We all know time cannot be reversed, meaning we have a limited amount of energy and resources before we die. If you really want to win in this game called life, you need to be asking the right questions. Really, the endgame is what your purpose is (refer to Chapter 10 on finding your purpose), and getting closer to the endgame will involve concrete decisions to strengthen the process.

When anyone encounters a situation they are unsure of,

we must think whether it's worth pursuing for the long haul. Otherwise, it's not that important. Simply, if you're certain about something, do it, or else you'll regret it in life when you're old, decrepit, and full of "I wish" moments.

The longer you leave something to get back to it at a later time (procrastination), the higher the chance it will be that you won't do it. Just keep in mind that even though your body will be aching for you to stop, it's just temporary pain (physical and mental). This pain hurts much less than looking into this moment a year from now and having more regret from not doing it.

Following are three examples of how regret-factoring is incredibly effective to SIMULATE THE BEST outcome:

1. SIGNING UP FOR A MARATHON. You may not be a runner nor have any inclination to take on this sport, but this is a goal for if you want to have a taste of true greatness. Forty-two-plus kilometers does sound like a big deal and it will even scare you a little. But something happens during the process of preparing for a marathon. The training will get you out of your comfort zone and in the right mindset. And you may even meet others who are on the same journey.

   Then comes race day. You will be riddled with fear, questioning why on earth you decided to take on this ridiculous idea, when in fact many others are there in the same situation as you. I'll guarantee you two things: the first one is that it will be one hell of an emotional, physical, and mental roller-coaster running these 42 km. The second is, you'll even come across periods where quitting will seem like the best option, but you won't quit. Why? BECAUSE YOU ARE A WARRIOR. You'll continue to run, and before you know it, you'll cross that finish line and be the happiest person in the world.

2. WORRYING ABOUT WHAT MY FRIENDS THINK OF MY BUSINESS. Here's the thing with democracy; the main pro is it's great if you're in a group situation needing a majority-vote decision like deciding where to go for lunch. But when it comes to your thinking, never be democratic. If your friends and family aren't supportive, it comes down to not letting their words dictate your thoughts and actions. At the end of the day, it's what *you* want! Your friends and family love you dearly, however, their input is only because it may not have worked for them or it's totally unnatural. If you listen, it'll put restrictions on your beliefs.

Instead, only listen to the 1 percent of those who can guide you, because they're the experts who have done it. Would you listen to some guy who killed it in business or to a friend who has only been an employee working for someone else's dream? You listen to the entrepreneur, because they understand the belief you have in yourself. It's the same for dating. Don't get your advice from a person who's been through a couple divorces. Seek that couple who has been through decades together and still loves each other after all the setbacks. When you change your health and body, don't listen to those who aren't eating the right foods, never exercise, or who are unfit. Get advice from health consultants with killer fitness, because they're doing something right.

If you're starting a business, listen to the 1 percent and make them part of your inner circle and life mentors as your decision trustees, otherwise, you'll always be unsure and will over-think every big decision with all the contradicting thoughts.

3. SUCCUMBING TO PEER PRESSURE TO DRINK OR PARTY. This one is simple. Don't feel obliged if a group of friends are egging you on to party with them. You have a purpose and end goal, and partying is not what you're striving for. It's okay to celebrate now and then, but if peer pressure is involved, think whether it'll get you toward your end goal. If it won't, then put a rain check on it. Remember, this is going be one long journey!

Regret-factoring is a great tool to ensure you take that crucial leap of faith. Sometimes, that leap of faith may only be a foot long when it seems to be a canyon distance apart. When Bill Gates and Paul Allen were building Microsoft, they felt the need to hire a CEO to be the face of the brand, and that's when Steve Ballmer came in. Gates persuaded Ballmer to leave Harvard during the company's early 1980s startup. He had to decide if he wanted to work for the technology giant. Ballmer saw this as a great opportunity, even though he didn't finish his degree. However, that probably didn't matter, since he had a net worth of $27 billion after retiring from Microsoft in 2014. I highly doubt Ballmer regretted leaving Harvard.

MIND HACK #5: ALWAYS THINKING YOU HAVE MORE THAN YOU DO

Whether you're running 42 km, working out for an hour, or launching a business, the hardest part is actually finishing the task. When running a full marathon, it seems to actually start around the 32 km mark when there's 30 percent of the race remaining. Believe it or not, for a 100 km ultramarathon the first 70 percent goes by pretty quickly—the distance isn't on your mind as much and you just accept that it's going to be a long day. That final 30 percent is when the mental and emotional side of things come into play and try to take over. At that point, what you want to do is automatically think you have more to do. That means, if you're running a 42 km marathon, tell yourself that you have 50 km to go; or if you're doing a 2 km swim, tell yourself you have 2.5 km to go. By always thinking you have more, it pushes back that 30 percent, so when it comes to that adversarial moment, it'll all be less of a mental wall by the time you reach the finish line. And have you ever noticed, when you just want to finish already, that's when you can't stop looking at the clock and wondering why time is going so slow. Try visualizing you are finishing an hour or two later and time will fly before you know it.

Subconsciously, you should be thinking you have more required than you actually do. This does take some practice, but it can be a very effective tool. It's simple but it's not easy!

MIND HACK #6: CONTRAST BIASING (PERSPECTIVE)

This is a cognitive bias that's incredibly handy (if used correctly) when completing any goal. Think about people who have done what you're already doing but at a much greater level. When you think in perspective, it will give you something to gauge your progress on. Just don't get confused with comparing your success to theirs, because they're on a different path. You're just noticing how, as humans, they've made it happen. Therefore, you can too. In our case with running, we often think of the Tarahumara Indians who can run 322 km at a time. If they can run 322 km, then we can do 42 km. Now I'm at the point of competing in 322 km races and longer.

A common question I get asked is, "Are you crazy?" My response is, "Well, kinda, but not that crazy."

If you're not used to being around the same people, then all these endurance events I am doing this year will seem a little extreme to you. However, when you compare it to the people who have risen to the top, then it makes my efforts look like a walk in the park.

It actually puts you back on earth when you think in perspective, because you have something to measure everything against for completing your goals. In my case, an example would be if Dean Karnazes (famous ultrarunner) can run fifty marathons in fifty days, then I can do thirty in one year. Or, if the Tarahumara can run 322 km in one go, I can run a 100 km ultramarathon. This style of thinking is called contrast biasing, which is a type of cognitive bias. Raising the bar is something I've been constantly working on.

Usually when you have a passion for something, you tend to look up to a specific someone or a handful of people as inspiration. In this case, Joe De Sena, the founder of Spartan Race has probably been my biggest influence and inspiration. In his book *Spartan Up!* And in a specific interview he did with London Real Academy, he teaches you how to be comfortable being uncomfortable and to deliberately go through purposeful suffering. If there's a marathon event on that day, I'll pick the furthest distance. If it's raining, I will still run. If I said we would run a 9 km training run, we will run 10 km. It pretty much makes you go that extra level to teach you how to have thick skin and not complain about the event.

The man is also a machine. In one week, he did the Vermont 100 marathon, the Badwater 135 marathon (world's toughest foot race), and the Lake Placid Triathlon. That makes you think, "If he can do that much in one week, I can sign up for a 160 km, which is only a third of what he had to push through in an entire week." Notice there was contrast biasing involved there?

PUSHING YOUR LIMITS

Following are several practical tips on what you can do today and this week to help you push your limits:

- In whatever industry or field you're in, think straight to the top and emulate what they've done to get where they are. Remember to not compare yourself to them as they're on a different journey.

- Travel if you haven't already. Go to places where there's culture shock (India, Brazil, Africa, etc.).
- If you're signing up for a 10 km run, sign up for the half-marathon or full marathon instead. Just try it to see if you can do it (which I'm sure you will).

What perspective thinking has taught me is that it can be applied to every pillar of life. If you're running a business, think of Elon Musk. The man started three companies simultaneously and each has at least $1 billion valuation. Therefore, you can start one business and make $1 million. If you want to gain muscle, think of Arnold Schwarzenegger. He trained six hours a day and won Mr. Olympia for eight years. Therefore, you can work out for one hour each day.

If you want to become happier, then it's important to travel and explore new cultures. With any developing third world country, you'll notice that in some villages or areas where there's poverty, the people living there have hardly any resources and everything is meager, or even worse. But the most profound thing is that they're the happiest people in the world. Why's that? Because they don't own anything materialistic and their entire lifestyle is simplified to what they need. It's also because they've gone through the stress which makes them grateful to have their families and surroundings.

This isn't about telling you not to own anything materialistic. Sometimes it's rewarding to have a big TV; however, if you're complaining about the car or clothes you don't have, just be grateful for what you've got already.

MIND HACK #7: NOT ACCEPTING FAILURE OR LETTING THE TEAM DOWN

What's worse than signing up for a race and struggling to get through it on a bad day? A DNF (did not finish) would have to be it. The fact that you went out of your way to pay for a run and put the time and effort in should drive you to finish the race. Having the feeling of loss aversion is one thing, but really use that fear of failure to help you push through. There's no better feeling than finishing a race after being so close to breaking down, but the best feeling comes when you realize you managed to stick with it and got to the finish line.

It's actually better to have at least given something a try and not come out with a win than to not try at all. Failure has negative connotations and it's automatically assumed the repercussions attached are going to embarrass you rather than do any good. That's when you look at every failure as an experiment that didn't go to plan. During Einstein's discovery of the famous $e=mc^2$ formula, he didn't get it the first time. Testing his hypothesis that he believed there was a mass-energy equivalence took him years of testing. Each test would get him closer to the answer, but whatever didn't work wasn't looked at as a failure. It was put to the side and simply perceived as misconstrued findings and the experiment didn't go as planned.

I know what it's like to have that many runs on the agenda. There seems to be some sort of doubt from people perceiving it's impossible. Or, more commonly, people just associate the word crazy with doing a marathon. They can't imagine signing up and training for it. This kind of feedback is actually a driving force to keeping me going. It means that I get to do something I love out of passion and curiosity, and if anyone thinks it can't be done, then it makes you work even harder for it. I may not be the fastest or the fittest runner in the community, but I'm definitely dedicated and constantly investing time and effort into myself to get better as each day goes by. Plus, these events I tackle are causes bigger than we are. The last thing I want to do is let the team down with any unsuccessful finishes.

MIND HACK #8: USING HATE-FILLED COMMENTS TO FUEL YOU TO THE FINISH (SILENCING THE HATERS)

We all have those groups of people who have nothing better to do than give off negative energy. They usually have nothing nice to say about completing your goals. You know what? Perfect! Hold every word they say and use them as your drive to push on. This kind of determination can be hard—keeping these people out of your head—but there's no better feeling than completing a marathon or ultramarathon when people said you couldn't do it!

This one really brings out the rebellion in us! It's one of the most gratifying feelings to prove someone wrong, especially when the majority didn't think it was possible. Obviously, respect their values and opinions, but don't let them dictate who you are or you'll start putting limits on your beliefs.

MIND HACK #9: SET LITTLE GOALS SO YOU CAN HAVE A TASTE OF VICTORY

One of the keys you may have noticed during this path to discovery is that any of these methods you choose to undertake are best accomplished through small steps that'll incrementally grow without you even realizing it. Think of the set of dominos, ranging in size from super small to gigantic. That big bastard at the end won't even budge until the first one is knocked over, and then the next one can't move until there's enough momentum. At first, when a task feels tough, then it works and you accomplish it, it doesn't feel like work anymore.

PRACTICAL EXAMPLES ON HOW TO INCREMENTALLY GROW WITH GOALS

- Maybe you have a book you want to publish in the next year but haven't really started. Practice writing 500 words a day, every day, and then you'll get into a cadence on being able to write hours on end.
- You want to lose 10 kg in weight. Focus on a few kilograms first so you can see that it's quite possible, and then aim to smash the rest out in bite-size chunks.
- You're not really into sports but you love to walk to stay active, but not at the level to hit the 10,000 steps a day mark just yet. Start at 3,000 steps and build up an extra 250 steps the next day. You'll reach the 10,000 steps with flying colors!

Then there are those who have decided to finally put on the running shoes and have their bodies go through hours of pain just to understand what a marathon feels like. I salute you! You're braver than most people! It makes things easier if you break your run into chunk-size pieces by setting little goals. For example, if you're running a 42 km marathon, aim for 10 km intervals or focus on getting to that lamp post that's a kilometer away. You'll get there before you know it, and then you just rinse-and-repeat the process until you've finished the race.

MIND HACK #10: HOLDING YOURSELF ACCOUNTABLE FROM LOSS-AVERSION

I know how it feels to be on the progressive train and one that's in a standstill position. I can tell you now that the first one is the one you want to be boarding. What happens when we stop eating right, stop training, and stop being uncomfortable? We stop growing and it's hard to get back into the habit of moving forward.

That's why it's absolutely vital to continue learning and training after taking on a twelve-week boot camp or booking the next event in advance. Too many participants think it's okay to be comfortable again and they disregard everything they've worked their asses for and all the training they dedicated themselves to. Welcome back to square one.

The endurance projects I've been part of since 2015 have been ones where I don't become complacent or get into a rhythm of relaxation for long stretches of time. I'm not saying not to recover, that's something completely different. What I'm saying is having an event always booked and ready in advance will keep your mindset in gear.

"Dude, how are you able to complete these twenty-four-hour challenges?" is a common question I get asked. Well, I look at every event as a training session for the next one and because each event is tied in with some altruistic cause, I'm doing it for a cause bigger than myself. What that does is shift my thinking to ensure I don't let the team down and I become focused on finishing, no matter what.

If you purchase anything in advance, you're more likely to do it because you don't want that feeling of loss-aversion. It's as if you're guilting yourself to get the job done, no matter what. Essentially, you're protecting yourself from yourself.

FINAL TAKE ON MIND HACKS

Be sure to remember these hacks that are designed as tools to propel you and fast-track the system to surpass the mental blocks. Like any new habit, learn to make them a new friend and be persistent at first. There will be plenty of times when you'll wonder if it's working, but like any muscle in the body, hustle the mind as a muscle too. The more you practice these with a reps-and-sets mentality, the stronger they'll become over time.

CHAPTER 9

WHY HEALTH SHOULD BE YOUR #1 PRIORITY

"The energy between this family [running community] and my internalization is morphed from sporadic murky bursts of smoke into a transparent cloud of euphoria. It's an exhilarating rush of abundance; prosperous wealth in my well-being and emotional engine, per se. There's a profound realization that arises, and my stomach has trimmed to the point where I can see bumps of tensed muscles after years of a tough grind that are known as abs to most. In fact, I am not astonished with the reconstructed gut, but as I look into the mirror, I see the face of a warrior with a six-pack mind more shredded than any Mr. Olympia contestant I've ever seen on TV." —March 13, 2017

Experiencing psychological torment narrowed my clarity, and I was treading on thin ice. Researching why I wasn't happy through multiple web links and books widened that clarity to keep me curious. Once I discovered I needed to make my health my #1 priority, that single-handedly saved my life.

YOU ARE WHAT YOU THINK AND CONSUME

As a person who's fascinated with human behavior and dynamics, it astounds me how there are people who set limits on themselves and those who are limitless. A healthy mind will always equate to healthy decisions; but to be able to have absolute focus, this is when you have to be careful about what you consume. That could be anything from the foods you eat, to the media you watch, to the people you constantly hang around with. You are a product of your environment.

Remember that we can't limit our thinking, and the **impossible** becomes **"I'M POSSIBLE!"**

I know for myself that when I consume large amounts of junk food and high-sugar snacks, my thinking is hazy and my brain feels like it's in a fog. Plus, the sugar will only make me hungrier because the dopamine in our brains reacts the same as we do with cocaine, believe it or not.

I know from my experience with cocaine that once I got hooked, it was all I craved. This was during my depressed state back in 2014. My mental state at the time had me feeling more alone than ever, and I didn't know any better at the time. When I look back at that time now, I realize I'm not the only person who succumbed to this coping mechanism. It's the perfect example of Simple Pain Avoiding Tendency, cognitive bias #11 in Chapter 4.

Constantly indulging in sugar-based snacks not only made me hungrier but my head was experiencing a rush that would have all pistons firing, subsequently red-lining until I was burned out. And if you're burned out, productivity isn't happening any time soon.

On average, every day we undergo three to five bursts of mental glycogen, which is essentially the thinking energy source to fuel any brain activity and logical decision making. When your brain is rushed at a max for too long, then your daily glycogen will surpass its normal limits and you'll feel tired of everything. It's so frustrating when you can't think!

I'm not telling you to quit eating sugar, but if you want progress, reduce the amount of refined sugars you intake. Maybe not all at once, but start small and eventually it'll be a piece of cake (sugar-free cake that is). Yes, it will be tough at first, but resist every urge to have a little. Before you know it, your cravings won't be dependent on sugar. Where sugar can have an effect on your mental ability, it can also affect you physically. It literally makes you hungrier, especially when it's a snack. If you eat more than normal, it can turn into a bad habit—to the point where your weight will slowly increase again and your self-confidence will back down.

If there's a chocolate in the fridge, it's easier to resist the temptation if I haven't been indulging in sweets because it's as if I've forgotten what I'm missing. I'm in the right zone with how I want my ideal body to look.

THE GREATEST INVESTMENTS IN LIFE ARE

1. Health, followed by
2. Social capital

The point of an investment is to deploy some sort of commodity at the beginning to have a better return; but importantly, you want an exponential return. What's the most valuable commodity on earth? No, it's not coffee or even cocaine; it's time. Think about it. You can regain money if you lose it, but you can't get back any lost time.

"If you don't look after your health, how are you meant to make good decisions in business and life?"

—RICHARD BRANSON

Fucking spot on, Richie!

But really, the biggest form of wealth is your health, in my opinion. I personally don't think wealth is just money when your life should be integrated with wealth, love, relationships, and happiness too.

How are we meant to live happy and purposeful lives if we're not waking up healthy each day? A part of the world puts a negative connotation on the word "healthy" and can define it as uncool. This is when you must realize that your perception on health shouldn't be affected by others, especially those who aren't experts in the field. Remember to not be democratic with your thinking! Do you know what's uncool? Not supporting your child's musical skills and ambitions because you won't fit in the seats after you stopped looking after your health.

You have access to thousands of health books on topics like diets and exercise, but they all have the same correlation to living a healthy life. That is, don't eat too many shitty foods, watch how much you're eating, and make sure you're moving everyday even if it's walking.

MAKING HEALTH #1 PRIORITY

GET OUTSIDE AND EXPLORE MORE

What's one of the best ways to start your day? Get outside and watch the sun rise. There's something magical in the sky with its changing colors, opening that blanket of warmth to recalibrate the mind for a new day. Even if it's once a week and you're texting a bunch of friends to meet for a run or hike, get out there early enough to really appreciate the sunrise. You'll feel like you've accomplished more in your day when you get started earlier.

Even if you're not up early, it's always a great idea to be outdoors. We are so consumed with social media that a break from it will probably do more good than harm. Go hiking, trail running, kayaking, paddle boarding, spelunking, or anything that involves you driving somewhere far enough to get away from your house and enjoy nature's backyard.

HEALTH SHOULD ALWAYS BE NUMBER ONE

From my experiences, I was able to benefit in several ways:

- Exercise will help you sleep. Even if you're an insomniac, after you get moving, you will become tired from a physical standpoint and you just want to pass out.
- All the endorphins and sweat released in my system got the right hormones pumping.
- Actually being able to think and not feel lethargic all the time is wonderful, because it happens when you start eating right.

- It can become a fun period to see how far you can push yourself when you notice your progress.
- It increases self-confidence to a point where you feel like a new person.
- When you become involved with a new community, you soon meet new people and become friends.

WHY SOCIAL CAPITAL IS YOUR SECOND GREATEST INVESTMENT (AFTER HEALTH)

"Network or No Work," is a saying that applies to growth, especially in business. Yet it can be just as effective in anything we face in life. If you only have a small group of allies, it restricts the amount of advocacy on both sides. That is, you can only get referred by your handful of connections.

Going back to Chapter 6 on collaboration, this method of building relationships will naturally increase your network. Put simply, your network is your net worth. Like building a friendship, this is the same method in network-building. You have to provide plenty of value because it's a two-way street. Subsequently, your network will naturally advocate you to their network. However, you have to be valuable. So, make yourself an asset that stands out and you'll experience a true network effect.

Network-building is the process of growing your relationships for advocacy and collaboration, whereas networking is often associated with being that person in the room who has a massive stack of business cards and throws them at everyone. If no one asked for your card, you're basically wasting their time and yours too. Only give your card to someone who asks for it, or else it's going straight in the bin because they won't remember who you are.

For extraverts, it's easy to make friends because they're the loudest people out there and often the life of the party. For introverts, talking with strangers and never-before-seen folk isn't the easiest of tasks. But this is where it probably pays to have friends who are extraverts so they can introduce you to people they know. Introverts may outwardly express they "hate people," but that's just the narrative they're telling themselves in their head. It's based on the fact that they deeply relate to feeling fearful and they're afraid they might have to make a connection with a total stranger.

At the end of the day, we humans are hardwired for connection and story, so it will naturally make us happier if we are surrounded by like-minded people and those who can help us grow (mentors). Mentors in particular can make us feel uncomfortable because we perceive them to have a higher level of experience, which we're hoping will rub off on us after plenty of encounters. Mentors are out there, but you have to be a relentless learning sponge and a valuable asset to attract these types of people to help build your network. However, mentors will immensely make your life easier to be advocated for.

CHAPTER 10

—

THE ACTUAL ENDGAME...LEGACY AND PURPOSE

"As the sun rises over the horizon, my body automatically responds before the alarm has a chance of greeting me with its screeching presence. Fully able to realize the purpose that's driving this once-restless soul into depths of vision, I'm tap-dancing out of the sheets. It's such a gift to have sheer clarity, and I can see the end goal and my god, she's beautiful." —June 27, 2017

"What do you want?" is a question made up of four simple words, but it's hard for 99.999 percent of the world's population to answer. If you can think with the endgame in mind, not only will you know what you want, but you'll have a clearer path to get you there, because it comes down to reverse engineering the outcome.

Why would you jump in the car and not know where to put the address in the GPS? The same thing applies to your life. When you know the end destination, you can work backward to make things simpler, especially when there's an uncertain time limit, like when you're going to die. You won't know when this will happen because it's an invariable constant. But you should be nimble with what you can do immediately. All you have to do is be patient with the process.

SO, HOW DO I FIND THE END GOAL (MY PURPOSE)?

It comes down to how you want to be remembered; it's your legacy.

Try this exercise: picture yourself dead, which could be in ten, twenty, or even sixty years. Let's assume you can see everyone showing up at your own funeral, with thousands or even millions of people mourning your death because you did great things. People have flown in from all over the country and across the globe and they have cancelled all commitments they had just to be at your funeral. Whoever has the honor of reading your eulogy has this very lengthy speech prepared, but what does it say? Were you remembered for humanitarian reasons or politics; where you someone who was incredibly giving, an amazing sport star, or even one of the top intellects who ever lived? Or were you someone who was just another average person where mediocrity took over and it was too late to do something about it? Well, this is where you get to decide!

The next three pages are blank on purpose. They are there for you to fill in your eulogy. I want you to get as specific as possible with how you want to be known, for your greatness. The more detailed your writing is, the clearer your purpose is. Make sure you really think this one through, because the last thing you want is to get a few years down the track and realize it's not what you truly wanted. Even if you're not entirely sure, write down the first thing that comes to mind. It should be something you can talk about endlessly and that gives you goosebumps thinking about it. Describe how great you'll be and, by doing that, you'll be on the right track.

From here, use this eulogy method to be your guide and accountability partner. Once it's handwritten, re-write it again, type it up, and read it every morning to remind you why you're alive, to serve your purpose. By re-writing and reading it over and over, it will help embed the message into your brain.

In a world of 7.5 billion people (and growing), you have to stick out from the rest, and why not be one of the greats who was purely known for being a game changer? If your goals and ambitions don't scare you, you're not thinking big enough. If you're stuck, then invert the question and ask yourself, "What don't I want to be known as when I die?"

"Be so good they can't ignore you."

—STEVE MARTIN

MY EULOGY SPEECH:

"Today, we've lost one of the greats. (Insert your name here) was known for many things...

....

....

....

....

....

....

....

....

....

....

....

....

....

....

....

....

....

....

....

....

....

....

....

....

....

....

....

....

....

....

....

Perfect, you know your end goal!

Note, as your progress moves ahead, so does your confidence. You will soon have the urge to strive for greatness. Yes, we most definitely have to aim big and set our standards high to get to the level where execution happens easily. For even the tasks that seem impossible must start small.

I've said it before and I'll say it again: remember that we can't limit our thinking. The **impossible** becomes **"I'M POSSIBLE!"** From here, you work backward until you can figure out your immediate daily goals that can drive you toward the end result.

IN ESSENCE, THIS IS HOW TO REVERSE ENGINEER LIFE

For me, everything I do is predicated on when I die, so I'm known as the "go-to guy on practical resilience," the thought leader who pushed the limits through endurance for other people. This is the vision which I know is going to take a bloody long time (decades), so I'm patient with this, but I'm impatient with the immediate daily goals I can do today to get me closer to this.

You may have finally figured out your purpose, and now you've become obsessed with it. That's good! You can't get stumped on deciding what you're good at any longer, because you know this field exceptionally well. Become a practitioner, an experimenter, and a mad scientist to get yourself curious so you fail quick. Fast-track your experience and knowledge along the journey.

Even when there's clarity with the vision you've mapped out above, the many bumps, setbacks, and stresses you'll encounter along the journey are inevitable. Things will be great and then, all of a sudden, an unforeseen event will arise like a death in the family or getting involved in a car crash. Well, that takes almost all the energy away from your vision and places it into the current situation. Some people will freak out, so you need to keep your composure. Yes, it will be normal to feel certain emotions, but you need to be cool under pressure. This is where you continue to practice specific mind hacks (Chapter 8) to deliberately immerse yourself in daily adversity and come out stronger so you're prepared in advance for any crisis.

A rule of thumb when it comes to life: don't be one of those wankers who strive for weekends and hates Mondays. If you're in this situation, you're probably in the wrong profession. That's what the rat race does. You'll be surrounded by workers who live in jobs they hate and their negativity will rub off on you. Life is too short to be doing what you don't enjoy.

REMEMBER, TIME IS FINITE AND MONEY CAN ALWAYS BE REGAINED

"But I need an income to pay bills, support my family, etc." The most practical way to live your dream is to have a side hustle. Have that project you've always wanted to do on the side and work on this every spare moment you have until you can figure out how to monetize it.

That means you must sacrifice every weekend, TV shows, and even deploy your energy after work. Working until midnight or 1:00 a.m. on this is not going to kill you. Yes, you'll be tired, but you'll be glad you put in the long hours when you see it turn to fruition.

If you have a boyfriend, girlfriend, or spouse, explain what you're doing and they'll understand. You can still see them, just schedule your time into this project after spending quality time with them. Or if it's easier, wake up a couple hours earlier and hustle your ass off before you go to work.

If you don't put in the work, you will never get the results. As I mentioned earlier, don't complain along the route to anyone, because it won't affect them and they won't care. This is only for you. Once there's some stability in this side income, that's when you make the move to get the fuck out of the place you hate working at!

Keep thinking that this extra work of maintaining the side hustle will be temporary! You just need the balls to get moving and have momentum. The last thing you'll be saying on your deathbed is that you wish it wasn't Monday. By then it's too late. So, keep this thought constantly on your mind.

When you start working on something that you enjoy every day, you don't know what day it is. That's exactly what you want! Thursday shouldn't feel any different than Monday. Your days should be in the mind of seasons. It's like how a farmer plants his crops in the summertime and then harvests in the winter. Apply the same concept so you put all the hard work in, and when it comes to Christmas time where no one wants to push anything forward, you can relax with friends and family.

For me, I usually wake up most mornings between 4:00 a.m. and 6:00 a.m., so I can get the most out of my day. And since I know my purpose in life, it has immensely increased my tap-dance-out-of-bed factor—but I don't literally tap dancing out of bed. This term is coined by billionaire investor Warren Buffett, who explains that when you have purpose and enjoy it, whatever you do for work or your pursuit in life, you'll get out of bed much much easier.

And of course, I make sure to have fun throughout this entire journey.

It's crazy how I've transformed from heavy depression and anxiety, feeling like I was in a lead mine 120 m underground that was about to collapse any minute, to becoming someone who is incredibly grateful and driven— in a disposition of feeling the ambience. I'm definitely out of the deeply dug rabbit hole and I've been shot into the stratosphere.

In space, there are no fences and borders.

IF YOU AIM HIGH IN WHATEVER YOU'RE DOING, YOU'LL BE SURPRISED AT HOW FAR YOU CAN GO

A great friend of mine who has extreme clarity and aims big is a gentleman named Andy Fell. I was introduced to Andy when he was the GM of Westpac, one of the big four banks of Australia. Over the years of knowing Andy, he has transitioned his career from the corporate life into the entrepreneur life.

"Looking at my life today, everything is great. I have clarity of purpose, I live my passion every day and I have both a wonderful lifestyle and incredible balance. I am also conscious that this is a moment in time, and life has a habit of throwing

curveballs at you when you least expect them. At these moments, we often cannot control what happens, we can certainly control how we respond. This is when our attitude, belief systems, and mindset matter most."

—ANDY FELL

Andy has explained to me that even during the very early years of his life, he was happy. He had loving, caring parents and siblings, always went to the same school in the same village, and had a great group of friends. Life felt simple in the days before computers, phones, and the internet. He lived in a time when he knew what he knew and he was sheltered from so much going on in the world.

He didn't have much money compared to those around him, but there was so much more.

The bit in the middle has been a mix of some wonderful times when everything was running smoothly. Life seemed a complete breeze to others when adversity and difficulty kicked in. It often seems in life that challenges like to turn up as a pack to attack you when you are in some way vulnerable.

While the details of these periods in Andy's life may be interesting to some, there was definitely a belief that what he learned is of value to all. When he was offered his first senior leadership role, he was relocated to a new part of the UK and placed in charge of a difficult and challenging business. It had underperformed its potential for a considerable period of time. As a young, energetic, determined, and passionate lad, he had a motility of running into brick walls. Some days he couldn't see and certainly didn't believe he was making any progress.

Then one day, a colleague came into his shared office and put an article down on the table in front of him. "Read this," the colleague said. That he did. The article was about rejecting mediocrity and the importance of focusing on the characteristics of a rhino on the charge as opposed to the cows chewing grass, contented in the meadows.

Subsequently, the more Andy thought about life, the more

he thought about the meaning of what he labelled "rhino rationale"—success is about pace, urgency, direction, and momentum. However, in challenging times particularly, it is also about resilience. It's the ability to persist, keep going, and push through. So, what helps?

"Optimism is true moral courage," a famous quote from Sir Ernest Shackleton who certainly knew how to succeed in difficult circumstances. Our attitude matters at all times, particularly when facing adversity. We also need to look for positive role models, mentors, friends, and colleagues. "Winners go to winners," and there's a strong correlating sense the reverse is true. Surround yourself with negative people with the attitude of a victim or a cynic and they will drag you down, unless you have incredible mental toughness.

A key to this is to continually focus on self-development and self-improvement. Andy is a great advocate of the more you learn about life and its challenges, the more important it becomes. It builds confidence, self-belief, and desire to stretch, push through challenges, and ultimately "soar to new heights." Linked to learning is the ability to journal frequently to capture thoughts, feelings, and emotions.

In his journal, he frequently wrote positive affirmations of "who I am and what I have/will achieve." The more he wrote and read his affirmations, the better he felt and the more confident he became to take the required action to move forward.

In addition to affirmation is visualization. Andy sees the world as he wants it to be. In essence, he dreams big! I truly believe our subconscious cannot tell the difference between perception and reality, so we need to feed it constantly with positives from our learning, affirmations, visualizations, and the people we surround ourselves with. This is so important, to be the "wind beneath our wings."

Andy is known for always carrying a tiny plastic rhino in his pocket to remind him of the need to keep going and to persist in whatever he is doing. Alongside the rhino is a small Yoda keyring telling him, "Do or do not. There is no try." These are Andy's symbols that bring him strength.

What do you carry?

WHEN YOU KNOW THE ACTUAL ENDGAME

Think about what matters most; think about where you want to be and who can help you get there. Think about both the end goal and the first step. If you fall, that's okay, but you can get up and you can keep going. There is always a light. See it getting slightly brighter each day with each action. Have belief.

CHAPTER 11

RESILIENCE IS THE GREATEST THING YOU CAN ACQUIRE IN LIFE

"Wow, I can't believe what a journey these past few years have been. I had dug a hole so deep, 'underground' was an understatement. It felt as if I was 120 meters below the surface in a collapsed lead mine and I really had to do something quickly or it would be too late. Emotionally, I've been through one hell of a roller-coaster ride; times seemed like the roller-coaster was buckling and about to be far from a smooth return to say the least. But you know what? I'm so fucking glad I went through this because I wouldn't be here today without those times. Falling into this field in such a unique way, I'm able to teach Practical Resilience to others helping them become mentally unbreakable. My appreciation and gratitude of life has immensely grown. It's as if I'm living a second life." —October 3, 2017

When all else fails, resilience is the only tool you'll have (and need) to help you bounce back when you fall. When any highly stressful scenario is about to occur, you will have your shit together. Why is resilience such an important characteristic to embed into yourself? Well, holistically, it'll prepare you for several crises, such as those listed in the following table.

HEALTH	FINANCE	RELATIONSHIPS	CAREER
20kg overweight and now apprehensive to work out	No savings and in at least $10k in debt	Finding out spouse or partner is cheating on you	Loss of job
Resorting to drugs and alcohol to deal with stress	Recession	Being betrayed by social circles	Business deal gone sour
Addicted to sugar or junk food	In need of $20k to start new venture	Death of a family member or close friend	Dealing with the entrepreneur life (i.e., the grind/no sleep)

"It doesn't matter how many setbacks you come across in life. It's your comeback that will make your story stand the test of time."

—TOFE EVANS

It doesn't matter how many times you fail and hit the ground hard, metaphorically speaking. What's important is how fast you get back up on your feet, despite how incredulous the fall was. Why are the greatest people perceived as if they're a type of god? Because they're resilient as fuck.

What would you think is sexier? Someone who complains about almost everything and melts down about every miniscule detail, OR someone who can take a loss so well that it's nothing to them. I hope you picked the latter.

It's part of the reason why I'm incredibly transparent in this book and in my keynotes with my falls and fails.

Profoundly, the most resilient show the most humility. The best speakers I've come across are people with such humility, it'll have you wondering how they've handled their losses. Like any habit, failures are built and encapsulated around a reps-and-set mentality where that warrior picks themselves back up every time.

There's definitely three people I look up to in particular who collaborate with me emotionally and have given me a reason to emulate their humility. Thus, when I captivate the attention of my audience, they can resonate with my story and the connection is so fucking concrete that I'll change their thinking for the greater good. Remember back at the start of the book, I said that humans are wired neurobiologically for connection and story.

THREE REMARKABLE FIGURES WHO CHANGED THEIR THINKING FOR THE GREATER GOOD

With these three public figures, I'll explain briefly what they're known for and how they've dealt with certain losses.

1. GARY VAYNERCHUK, FOUNDER OF VAYNERMEDIA

A public figure who's quite prevalent in the social media game is Gary Vaynerchuk, a.k.a Gary Vee. Gary is acknowledged for his "no bullshit" hustle and mentality and is appealing to say the least. He grew up as an immigrant from the former Soviet Union. After flunking high school, he chose to work in his family's wine business. Later, he helped it turn from $5 million to $60 million in yearly revenue in the space of five years.

Later on, he started Vaynermedia, a digital marketing agency for Fortune 500 brands emanating from several millions in revenue every year and into eight to nine figures a year. So, where he's been a big player in the entrepreneurial world, he's notoriously known for being involved as an angel investor and an early adopter in thriving brands like Twitter, Facebook, and Tumblr.

One deal he missed out on was Uber, the gigantic ride-sharing app that's destroyed the taxi industry. And it wasn't just once he passed on seed funding, it was twice he declined Uber's offer. If he took that deal, let's just say his current net worth would be much, much greater.

Gary is well aware that he was a fool to make the mistake of passing on Uber twice, but he's stoked he has this as a loss. In many interviews, he takes it like a fucking champ and is hungrier to win.

2. LEWIS HOWES, NYT BEST-SELLING AUTHOR AND FOUNDER OF THE SCHOOL OF GREATNESS

If you've been injured, you know how disheartening it

can be. Your schedule is completely disrupted and it feels like you're moving in a backward direction. That's exactly how Lewis Howes would've felt when he was living on his sister's couch for a year and a half while in a cast.

Who is Lewis Howes? Lewis is an athlete, entrepreneur, founder of the famous podcast known as *The School of Greatness*, and a NYT best-selling author with his book also called *The School of Greatness* and *The Mask of Masculinity*.

Lewis used to play college football and was trying to make it into the NFL until he got injured. When he couldn't play anymore, he had to live in a cast and had to rethink his future.

Lewis's story got my attention when he got himself out of that adversity and was able to continue a sporting career. He made a slight transition from American football to making the USA National Handball Team aiming to represent his country in the Olympics!

But his journey leading up to where he is now was nowhere near an easy ride. On top of having dealt with struggles with school life, sexual abuse had created such a dark presence that he resented those around him and suppressed his emotions until he understood the power of vulnerability. He not only catapulted himself out of this rut, but he helped many others, especially men who didn't think it was right to divulge and express feelings.

Despite having come across several obstacles along the way, with his professional football career ending in little more than a heartbeat, he tried to figure things out during those dark, depressing days. He lived on his sister's couch for a year and a half, and he managed to rise above the turmoil and inspire many others including myself. With his podcast, he interviewed some of the greatest minds and helped listeners strive for greatness.

3. JOE GEBBIA, CO-FOUNDER OF AIRBNB

A story that'll always have my attention is how Airbnb was able to turn an idea into a business with a $30 billion-plus valuation. This is the largest accommodation chain in the world that owns no real estate. Where Marriott is worth approximately $20 billion, it's astounding how many hotels they've had to build and how much staffing overhead they've had to deal with to get them where they are. Though Airbnb has been around for a fraction of the time and with an extraordinarily smaller team of 200, they are worth substantially more, which is astonishingly fascinating.

Originally, they created the idea of crowd-sharing when Joe and his co-founder, Brian Chesky, decided to host strangers as guests to help pay their rising San Francisco rent bill. This was a problem at first that has been innovated into a business model.

In their ten-year journey, it's been full of ups and downs, especially in the third year when company funding was starting to dry up. They tried setting up meetings with ten of the top venture capitalists of Silicon Valley and not one of those VCs agreed to lend any seed funding. Mainly because the idea at the time of allowing strangers to rent your house or rooms may have been perceived as a red-flag, with the words "stranger danger" attached to their company's name.

During his keynotes, Joe explains so beautifully how his team had undergone the Visa Round, (maxing out credit cards and putting each one into baseball card folders). They were $20,000 in debt and the guys needed to think of something quick or else their startup might bust, despite their proven success. But then something magical happened amidst the 2008 election. Joe and Brian were coming toward dire straits, but innovated out through sheer creativity. Their great idea was to incorporate a closer connection between hosts and guests, and the idea of having presidential cereal would pass as an idea to fund the business: *Obama-O's and Captain McCains.*

Their office turned from startup incubator to cereal production line after a massive influx of orders, even when they were sold for $40 per box! The cereal made headlines across CNN, Tech Crunch, and morning shows, increasing their demand to 500 boxes overnight. They instantly went from $20,000 in debt to miraculously breaking even in financial distress.

The cereal saga and Visa Round were only a couple scenarios of what Joe humbly explains during the rise of Airbnb, to the point he can shrug those moments in time away as not failures but feedback.

OBTAINING COURAGE FROM OTHER STORIES

After hearing about these pivotal moments with these three guys, it's clear how much courage was attained during tough times. If you want a really practical tool available to you each night before going to sleep that helps you naturally and undoubtedly grow courage, read biographies and memoirs. Not only will you be inspired and realize these "super-people" are also human beings like you and I, but when the person in the book has lived a fun, wild, successful, and interesting life, then it shows that anyone can do it. Which is part of the reason why I do these tough and extreme endurance events. There's always someone who's completed a tougher challenge.

You might recall the read-hack I mentioned in Chapter 5, the Blinkist app that provides a summary of any nonfiction book in a fifteen-minute read. I highly recommend using this app to save you hours of time getting that gold nugget of what the book's about. But my belief on reading biographies and memoirs should involve reading a great deal of their stories in detail so you can observe the process they endured. Otherwise, it'll seem as if they're an overnight success. You might as well hear about their story from the news, diminishing the true courage you can obtain from their journey with all the highs and the lows.

Everyday people give famous athletes, celebrities, and any high-profile person an insane amount of abrogating flack because they live in fancy houses with lavish lifestyles. To them, it's sexy in the eyes of the media to only explain the perfunctory of their success, often only the end result, when really they forgot to mention all the years of hard fucking work, their dedication and grinding when they believed what they had was going to be the next big thing. And it did, because their actions and results speak for themselves.

You'll always have some hero who will say, "Oh, yeah, Kobe Bryant gets treated like a god and has his own statue." Well, sorry to burst your bubble, bro, but Kobe was one disciplined motherfucker who got up at 3:00 a.m. every morning and worked on his jump shot for twenty-plus years while you were binge-watching every series on Netflix or partying till the early hours of the morning.

Instead, quit disparaging the hard workers and start applying discipline and dedication into your mindset that you're obsessing into the right fields. I'm not saying you're not a hard worker, but you have to be patient because your time will come! Hey, it took J.K. Rowling fifteen years before Harry Potter was a global success. Robin Williams spent years at bars and small comedy clubs before becoming recognized as a renowned comedian. Nelson Mandela spent twenty-seven years in prison for his protesting before becoming the greatest leader of South Africa. Your time will come, just keep working on your craft while those other people are playing it easy.

You may hate reading books and that's fine, but just listen to the audio version. From a NLP (neuro-linguistic programming) perspective, you have the audio-dominant types that respond quintessentially to sound; reading books might not be the best medium to soak in knowledge, yet listening to them would. Some of you travel at least an hour to work every day, and instead of listening to music, listen to an audiobook and it'll be finished within a week or so. The beauty of audiobooks is that you can control the speed to have it completed quicker.

Everyone makes mistakes, but they don't have to be yours. Not only will this shave years off the learning curve, but it's less fatal.

SOME OF THE BEST BIOGRAPHIES I'VE READ (IN NO SPECIFIC ORDER)

1. *Unbroken*—Biography of Louis Zamperini by Laura Hillenbrand
2. *Total Recall*—Autobiography of Arnold Schwarzenegger
3. *Elon Musk*—Biography of Elon Musk by Ashlee Vance
4. *Spartan UP!*—Autobiography of Joe De Sena
5. *No Hero*—Autobiography of Mark Owen
6. *When I Stop Talking, You'll Know I'm Dead*—Autobiography of Jerry Weintraub
7. *I Am Zlatan*—Autobiography of Zlatan Ibrahimovic
8. *Losing My Virginity*—Autobiography of Richard Branson
9. *The World I Live In and Optimism*—Biography of Helen Keller
10. *Life Without Limits*—Autobiography of Nick Vujicic

HOW RESILIENCE WAS THE MISSING KEY I NEEDED

Going back to my story at the start, I was putting my body through three coping mechanisms to ease my mental health struggles: (a) self-infliction, (b) hard drugs and alcohol, and (c) prescribed medication, but none were working and I wasn't sure if I'd escape this rabbit hole. So, what did I do? I started researching why I wasn't happy and I kept coming across the same pattern where my health had deteriorated to such an extent that I needed to make it my #1 priority. To be honest, I thought I was just a little messed up in the head, unaware what mental health was. I merely thought it was a term people would throw around, but later I learned that focusing on my physical health via endurance was curing me mentally as well as emotionally.

Holistically, that outlook put all the other important life pillars into place. My relationships with girls and overall network has been a hundred times stronger, my work life has vision and purpose now, and where I lacked in gratitude and happiness, it has grown immensely because I'm very appreciative of what's happened. I figured I had to take on a sport I enjoyed and that's how I started running. There was no chance I'd be taking up ball sports when my hand-eye coordination was horrendous. Running was an escapism, but it kept me distracted from my inner demons in such a good way I was able to use them to my advantage. My determination drove me to complete multiple extreme endurance challenges.

One challenge in particular was when I was in the Himalayas, as mentioned earlier, running an ultramarathon on the infamous Mt. Everest. It was the world's highest ultramarathon and one of the world's most dangerous, because you don't play around with high altitude. What I'd expect to finish in ten hours took us eighteen hours. The distance was never the problem, the high altitude was. It felt like breathing through a straw with our lungs failing and heart rates maxed out the entire race. By the end of the event, going downhill was a strenuous quad and knee workout, and uphill just thrashed the hell out of the lungs and heart. Plus, you can't pull out. There was no phone reception, and it's an expensive call out to get a helicopter if you can somehow get one to arrive.

Not only was I one of less than one hundred people to ever finish this ultramarathon on the world's highest mountain, but I was fortunate enough to dedicate this to a cause known as Cystic Fibrosis. I went into deeper detail earlier in the book, but for those who forgot, it's a multi-organ respiratory issue where it's hard for CF patients to breathe on a daily basis. And where it's hard to breathe on Everest from that high altitude, it gave me a great reason to help raise funds and awareness for a disease that's still looking for a cure.

Even though things were at an all-time low back in 2014, it's been quite the transformation since. After sharing my experience and the valuable lessons learned in the past few years, I know that the mental health dilemma can be simply fixed through what I call Practical Resilience.

A recent event I attended involved a new type of ultra-endurance. It was a double marathon, 80 km on a stand-up paddleboard. Why? To stand up for the youth of today, the ones who are having it tough and battling any sort of adversity. By demonstrating that to grow resilience, a concrete method is achieved through grit and facing fear straight on. By standing up for them, I was literally standing up the entire time, on a paddleboard, over an enduring distance.

IT ALL COMES BACK FULL CIRCLE

Do you remember my friend, Jake, whom I mentioned at the start of this book—he had battled with anxiety throughout his high school days? Well, he is a great example of how he broke the system as well. Luckily, he was fortunate enough to be introduced to running by his brother, not long after I was immersed in the endurance community.

A common method uses escapism and it is incredibly effective. It's exactly what I did. In his words, "It's the happiest I've been since I can remember." In the running community especially, you meet all these amazing people who are out to transform their lives from all the hurt they've experienced. You quickly realize you aren't alone and everyone is out to help each other. It's amazing what opening up and wanting to do something about it will do for the human psyche.

As well as hearing Jake's story, I've met grown-ass men almost twice my size open up to me, and it's even tougher for guys because we have all this testosterone embedded in us. There's a shield of macho that makes us feel it's better to hide emotions than express them.

As for Michael Phelps, he reached out for help when he was struggling big time. He said, "It was good for me to understand it's okay to not be okay. For me, it was hard to put my hand out and ask for help. That's the one thing that probably single-handedly changed my life and saved my life." Regrowing his resilience, he returned to the pool and competed in the Olympics at Rio, one last year, bringing in another four gold medals. Those wins raised his tally to a record-breaking twenty-three Olympic gold medals. Even with all the setbacks, the comeback is what'll make the story a great one, and this is a perfect example of it.

As for Thorpey, the Australian swimming legend, he opened up about his sexuality and chronic depression in 2014, saying, "Although it may have taken me awhile to get to this point and realization in my life, I assure you it's worth it." Both Olympians have been through very dark times in their lives. It's amazing how well they've grown into warriors both on and off the field.

For everyone here, we can all do things that would strengthen our mental resilience so we're unbreakable and grateful during those moments, in case we get heartbroken or lose a family member or even have a limb removed. What would you do today if you were given the opportunity to have strength resilience? I've given many practical tips in each chapter, though one way I'd highly recommend would be to start small and try training for 9 or 10 km (or a half-marathon if you're up for the challenge). For a cause greater than yourself that means a lot to you, and I promise you, it will be a bumpy process, but you'll come out happier, stronger, and grateful for it.

I've completed crazy feats like running 162 km in twenty-four hours around a 400 m track, being locked in high altitude chambers for forty-eight hours for university studies, running an ultramarathon on Mt. Everest, and was even nominated for the 2017 Young Australian of the Year—all the events and accolades I've accumulated these past few years have been great and eye-openers to say the least. However, my proudest moment is how I've overcome all my mental health struggles and conquered my mind.

To me, that is my greatest achievement.

Thank you for reading and I truly hope this book will be of immense value to you. Please continue to turn the proceeding pages to get in touch with me!

GET IN TOUCH
WITH TOFE

Congratulations for making it to the end of this book. It's been quite a journey, hasn't it? And I hope you've highlighted and noted what you could do as action steps throughout each chapter. Hey, books aren't sacred items, so it's okay to pen your input on any of the pages.

I would really appreciate it if you bought a copy of this, as 10 percent of what you contributed goes to the LIVIN Org with a program to help the current mental health situation in Australia (and globally). There is a stigma about how it's okay to suppress your emotions, when in fact, it's creating the opposite—a destructive effect.

Remember, this book is designed to be your resilience bible so you can keep honing in on what are to be your new habits, which will later become skills. Your character traits will be noticed by strangers when you make a first impression and they want to learn from YOU!

If you'd love to work with me through either coaching or having me speak at your event, or you'd like to discuss a collaboration of some sort, please contact me via tofe@tofe-evans.com and be sure to follow me and say hi on social media. My handles are listed below.

If you loved *Everyone Has a Plan Until Sh!t Hits the Fan*, please give it a share on social media and tag me with the handles above and use the hashtag #PracticalResilience. You can leave a review on on Amazon.com.

ACKNOWLEDGMENTS: A SPECIAL THANKS

Originally, I was journaling my endurance experiences about how I was able to unfold my true self throughout the process, transforming this book project and encapsulating it into an understanding of mental health. I wanted to simplify a perception for others who were experiencing the perils I had been through. This has taken me the last year and a half to write, and I'm proud to see how it's turned to fruition. I became curious, hungry, and devoted and wanted to understand why I was experiencing such oppression. I wanted to learn how I could overcome the greatest mental obstacles I'd ever faced; and even more than that, I wanted to know how it could benefit every other person in this world who was experiencing the same thing.

But I couldn't do this without thanking a few people. Firstly, my Mum and Dad—Maria 'Joy' Evans and Murray

Evans. You guys have provided such an amazing amount of support, especially during my darkest days. I'm incredibly blessed to have you both by my side. You were there when I was at my worst and did what you could to propel me at my best. Showing up to my events and cheering me on, even if I was on the other side of the world—you are my biggest fans. To have both of my parents be caring, beautiful souls is more than I could ever ask for.

Then there's all the mental health experts, psychologists, neuroscientists, and behavioral scientists whom I've personally met to shed some light on a few topics, excavating the science out of certain behaviors that got me curious. These behaviors were pivotal and momentous junctures I had felt from the highs and lows. A special mention to Dr. Jodie Bradnam in particular within this field of experts. A PhD in Clinical Psychology, Dr. Bradnam admirably understands the brain and human connection. She's is a very kind-loving and genuine person who has spent a great deal of her time assisting me, validating the psychology behind my convictions and beliefs from my journey, which I've translated into this book. I couldn't do this one without you, so I thank you with all my heart.

Then there's my endurance partner and one of my best friends, Antony Sedman. We've been on this endurance journey of The Wounded Pelicans from the start and it's blossomed into a companionship along the way. Little did

I know that all this endurance would fix me mentally. I truly did take on this project with you as our aim was to get fit and help others. Throughout this entire process, it's created so much opportunity for us, including traveling to many parts of the world, while pushing the limits for others.

Lastly, I want to thank those who have supported me in any way, shape, or form. There are those who only know me from my days of distress. There are those who know me from some sort of endurance, and there are those who are only finding out about me now. Not to mention all the mentors and great friends I've met throughout this adventure, who saw something special in me and believed in what I envisioned. Thank you!

All of you amazing people are my fuel, and I am humbled to have you along for this ride.

Thank you and I truly hope this book made an impact on you.

Tofe

REFERENCES

A Free DISC Personality Test: Gain Insights to Build
Better, Stronger, More Fulfilling Relationships." DISC
Personality Testing. Accessed January 20, 2018, https://
discpersonalitytesting.com/free-disc-test/.

"About Cystic Fibrosis." Cystic Fibrosis Australia. Accessed November
20, 2016. http://www.cysticfibrosis.org.au/all/about-cf/.

Borges, Philipe. "Will Smith Running and Reading—Key to Life
Success Speech." Motivateamazebegreat.com. Accessed April
18, 2015. http://www.motivateamazebegreat.com/2014/03/
will-smith-running-and-reading-key-to.html.

Brous, Kathy. "Dan Siegel on Explicit Memory."
AttachmentDisorderHealing.com. June 27, 2014. http://
attachmentdisorderhealing.com/daniel-siegel-2/.

Carmichael, Chris. The Karnazes Effect." Runner's World. January
3, 2007. https://www.runnersworld.com/runners-stories/
dean-karnazes-runs-50-marathons-in-50-days.

Evans, Brian D. "Most CEOs Read a Book a Week. This Is How
You Can Too (according to This Renowned Brain Coach)."
Business Books, Inc.com. June 27, 2017. https://www.inc.com/
brian-d-evans/most-ceos-read-a-book-a-week-this-is-how-
you-can-too-according-to-this-renowned-.html.

Evans, Tofe. "How to Be a Spartan with Spartan Race Founder—Joe Desena." The Wounded Pelicans. April 14, 2017. https://www. thewoundedpelicans.com/joe-desena/.

Fang, Dan. "Having Blown It on Uber, Investor Gary Vaynerchuk Shares His Lessons on How to Spot the Next "Unicorn." Business Insider, Australia. July 30, 2015. https://www.businessinsider.com.au/ gary-vaynerchuks-lessons-learned-on-uber-investment-2015-7.

"Free Personality Test." Neris Type Explorer. 16Personalities. Accessed March 27, 2015. https://www.16personalities.com/ free-personality-test.

Gardner, Ben D. "Busting the 21 Days Habit Formation Myth." Ucl.ac.uk., University College London. June 29, 2012. http://blogs.ucl.ac.uk/bsh/2012/06/29/ busting-the-21-days-habit-formation-myth/.

Goyal, Rohit, MD, Samia Qazi, MD, Laurie Ward, MD, Qazi Qaisar Afzal, MD, Mir Mustafa Ali, and Klaus-Dieter Lessnau, MD, FCCP. "High-Altitude Pulmonary Edema." Medscape, emedicine.medscape.com. December 31, 2015. https:// emedicine.medscape.com/article/300716-overview.

Graham, David A. "Rumsfeld's Knowns and Unknowns: The Intellectual History of a Quip." The Atlantic. March 27, 2014. https://www.theatlantic.com/politics/archive/2014/03/ rumsfelds-knowns-and-unknowns-the-intellectual-history-of-a-quip/359719/.

Hamblin, Abby. "Hurricane Harvey: 7 Inspiring Acts amid Dire Texas Flooding." The Conversation. The San Diego Union-Tribune. August 29, 2017. http://www.sandiegouniontribune. com/opinion/the-conversation/sd-hurricane-harvey-rescues-inspiring-acts-20170829-htmlstory.html?amp;i10c.ua=1.

"Hebbian Thoery." Science Direct, sciencedirect.com. Accessed June 23, 2017. https://www.sciencedirect.com/topics/ neuroscience/hebbian-theory.

Historian. "Bill Gates—Before He Was Famous." i-programmer. April 14, 2015. http://www.i-programmer.info/history/ people/606-bill-gates.html.

Howe, Lewis. "What Sharing My Childhood Rape Taught Me about Being a Loving, Vulnerable, Free Man." Lewishowes.com. Accessed March 19, 2017. https://lewishowes.com/podcast/ what-rape-taught-me/.

"Ian Thorpe Reveals He Struggled with Depression Since Teenage Years, Urges Others to Get Help with Mental Health." ABC. net.au. Updated February 18, 2016. http://www.abc.net.au/ news/2016-02-18/ian-thorpe-reveals-mental-health-issues-a-problem-since-teens/7180702.

Munger, Charlie. "Cognitive Bias." 25 Cognitive Biases.com. Accessed February 24, 2015. http://25cognitivebiases.com/.

Muto, Jordan. "'I Didn't Want to Be Alive': Michael Phelps Talks about Struggle with Depression." Today.com. December 13, 2017. https://www.today.com/health/michael-phelps-struggle-depression-mental-health-issues-t119969.

Myers, Wyatt. "7 Great Exercises to Ease Depression." Everyday Health. Rev. Lindsey Marcellin, MD, MPH. Updated September 25, 2014. https://www.everydayhealth.com/depression-pictures/great-exercises-to-fight-depression.aspx#01.

Nomura, Tadashi, Yasunori Murakami, Hotishi Gotoh, and Katsuhiko Ono. "Reconstruction of Ancestral Brains: Exploring the Evolutionary Process of Encephalization in Amniotes." Science Direct. *Neuroscience Research* 86: 25–36. https://doi. org/10.1016/j.neures.2014.03.004.

Pogue, John M. "Review of Michael Moss's *Salt Sugar Fat: How the Food Giants Hooked Us.* Ney York: Random House, 2013." *Baylor University Medical Center* 27, no. 3: 283–284, mcbi.nlm.nih.gov. July 27, 2014. https://www.ncbi.nlm.nih.gov/pmc/articles/PMC4059590/.

Roenigk, Alyssa. "Veteran and Hopeful Paralympian Ennis on the Power of Sports." ESPN Olympic Sports. June 30, 2017. http://www.espn.com/olympics/story/_/page/espnwbodyennis/mountaineer-wounded-warrior-kirstie-ennis-long-road-recovery-body-2017.

"Ta-Da! The Launch of My Quiz on the Four Tendencies. Learn about Yourself!" Gretchen Rubin. January 14, 2015. https://gretchenrubin.com/2015/01/ta-da-the-launch-of-my-quiz-on-the-four-tendencies-learn-about-yourself/.

"Tenzing-Hillary Everest Ultra 60k." Great Himalaya Marathons. Accessed April 22, 2016. http://greathimalayamarathons.com/everest-ultra-marathon/.

Townsend, Tess. "How Novelty Cereal Helped Dig Airbnb Out of the 'Trough of Sorrow.'" Wire, inc.com. October 18, 2016. https://www.inc.com/tess-townsend/airbnb-gebbia-trough-of-sorrow-npr.html.

Upton, Louise. "Katrina Webb." Ruby.Connect.com.au. July 3, 2012. http://rubyconnection.com.au/insights/women-in-business/katrina-webb.aspx.

Urist, Jacoba. "What the Marshmallow Test Really Teaches about Self-Control." The Atlantic. September 24, 2014. https://www.theatlantic.com/health/archive/2014/09/what-the-marshmallow-test-really-teaches-about-self-control/380673/.

"What Are the 7 Most Powerful & Effective NLP Techniques on the Planet?" nlp.com. Accessed July 29, 2017. http://www.nlp.com/whatisnlp.php.

"What Is Emotional Intelligence?" Institute for Health and Human Potential, ihhp.com. Accessed September 24, 2015. https://www.ihhp.com/meaning-of-emotional-intelligence.

Zhenghao, Chen, Brandon Alcorn, Gayle Christensen, Nicholas Eriksson, Daphne Koller, and Ezekiel J. Emanuel. "Who's Benefiting from MOOCs, and Why?" *Harvard Business Review*. September 22, 2015. https://hbr.org/2015/09/whos-benefiting-from-moocs-and-why.

Passionate vs Companionate relationships - From *The Happiness Hypothesis: Finding Modern Truth in Ancient Wisdom* by Jonathan Haidt copyright © 2005. Reprinted by permission of Basic Books, an imprint of Perseus Books, LLC, a subsidiary of Hachette Book Group, Inc.

ABOUT THE AUTHOR

TOFE EVANS is constantly reinventing himself. His firm belief in pushing the boundaries of what the human body and mind are capable of inspired him to run a race down the slopes of Mt. Everest, and he has been called "crazy" on more occasions than he has been referred to by name. The endurance career he embarked upon in recent years not only shaped his character; it literally saved his life. He has become a powerful advocate for everyone's ability to rise above personal turmoil by conquering their own mind.

NOTES

....

....

....

....

....

....

....

....

....

....

....

....

....

....

....

....

....

....

....

....

....

....

....

....

STRESS AND ADVERSITY ARE INEVITABLE NO MATTER WHAT AGE YOU ARE. TOFE'S STORY IS A MUST-READ FOR ANYONE. HE IS A WONDERFUL EXAMPLE OF HOW YOU CAN USE PRACTICAL TOOLS TO DEVELOP RESILIENCE AND LIVE AN EXTRAORDINARY LIFE."

-KATRINA WEBB | OAM TRIPLE PARALYMPIC GOLD MEDALIST

Sh!t can happen to anyone, whether it's a life-threatening situation, a death in the family, a business gone bust, or another high-stress personal catastrophe. This book is your lifeline, offering tools to help you prepare yourself mentally to weather every impending storm.

Everyone Has a Plan Until Sh!t Hits the Fan is your Practical Resilience Bible. Tofe Evans provides the battle-tested mental artillery you need to escape the trenches under heavy fire and find your way onto safer ground. No matter what the crisis, his powerful insights and strategies will enable you to face every onslaught, survive any trauma, and ultimately emerge victorious.

Being ready for whatever the world throws at you is key. Adversity is a fact of life, and dealing with traumatic events requires calm, focus, and mental toughness and sharpness. Tofe Evans will get you there.

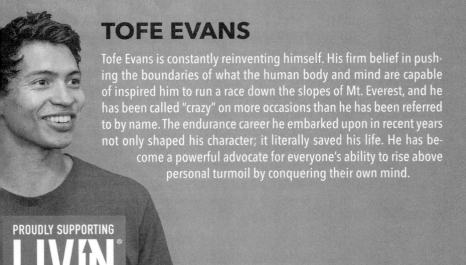

TOFE EVANS

Tofe Evans is constantly reinventing himself. His firm belief in pushing the boundaries of what the human body and mind are capable of inspired him to run a race down the slopes of Mt. Everest, and he has been called "crazy" on more occasions than he has been referred to by name. The endurance career he embarked upon in recent years not only shaped his character; it literally saved his life. He has become a powerful advocate for everyone's ability to rise above personal turmoil by conquering their own mind.